Effectiveness of Enterprise Risk Management

Izabela Jonek-Kowalska

Effectiveness of Enterprise Risk Management

Determinants and Opportunities for Improvement

palgrave
macmillan

Izabela Jonek-Kowalska
Silesian University of Technology
Gliwice, Poland

ISBN 978-3-030-95375-1   ISBN 978-3-030-95376-8 (eBook)
https://doi.org/10.1007/978-3-030-95376-8

This Palgrave Macmillan imprint is published by the registered company Springer Nature Switzerland AG.
The registered company address is: Gewerbestrasse 11, 6330 Cham, Switzerland

Preface

Risk management has been and continues to be a frequent topic in management and economics references. The various stages of risk management come under increasing scrutiny, including threats identification and assessment, and risk mitigation and control. Numerous publications are available on the design of complex enterprise risk management systems. However, very little research and consideration have been given to the effectiveness of implemented management solutions. Effectiveness in this context is understood as the achievement of the main objectives of risk management, which primarily include minimizing threats and losses to enable the survival and growth of the company.

There is therefore no comprehensive answer to the question of what factors contribute to the fact that risk is more or less effectively reduced? Meanwhile, competence in this area would certainly be useful in the process of improving management tools and systems both in theory and practice. All the more so as the factors that influence the results of risk management are diverse and consist of the following determinants: behavioral (related to the individual characteristics of decision-makers), endogenous (related to the inside of the company), and exogenous (related to the environment).

Bearing in mind the above circumstances, this monograph seeks answers to the following research problem: *What factors affect the effectiveness of risk management and how can they be prioritised?* For this problem to be solved, the monograph was divided into two parts. The first includes four theoretical chapters in which previous literature and research on risk management in the enterprise are reviewed and the effectiveness of this process is assessed. The second, also consisting of four chapters, contains the methodology and results of research on the assessment of the effectiveness of risk management in practice. The research was carried out on a representative sample of 722 Polish large and medium-sized enterprises.

The main purpose of the research, in direct reference to the research problem, was to identify the determinants of the effectiveness of risk management and to assess the strength of their impact on the degree of achievement of risk management objectives. The sub-goals were formulated as follows:

- Selecting and characterising individual groups of determinants of risk management in the enterprise
- Determining possible cause and effect relationships between groups of determinants and the effectiveness of risk management.
- Translating the model assumptions into a set of questions addressed to enterprises.
- Statistical determination of the sample size to ensure that it is representative.
- Obtaining basic statistical information on risk management in the surveyed enterprises.
- Examination of the strengths and the direction of multidimensional dependencies in the developed research model.
- Confrontation of the research results with previous theoretical and practical observations.
- Development of recommendations for the improvement of risk management in practice.

The above mentioned intentions are consistently and systematically implemented in eight chapters of this monograph.

The distinguishing feature of this publication is the reference of its content exclusively to the aspect of effectiveness of enterprise risk management. Focusing on this problem guarantees the uniqueness of the content and in-depth analysis of a narrow rarely described aspect of risk management. Furthermore, this issue is important both from a theoretical and practical point of view. The advantage of the book is also the use of the results of research conducted on a large group of enterprises and the development of the author's universal model for assessing the effectiveness of enterprise risk managers.

Given the above, the distinguishing features of this book include:

- to fill the research gap in the assessment and determinants of enterprise risk management effectiveness;
- to develop a theoretical and practical overview of considerations and research on risk management effectiveness from an international perspective;
- to adopt a multifaceted approach to the assessment of risk management effectiveness taking into account behavioral, endogenous, and exogenous factors;
- to present the results of research carried out on a representative group of 722 companies on the determinants of risk management effectiveness;
- to formulate universal conclusions and recommendations for improving tools and systems of enterprise risk management, particularly important in the context of the economic crises that companies are currently facing whose effects will have to be mitigated in the upcoming years.

This monograph is addressed primarily to academics and practitioners involved in risk management. It can also be successfully used as a textbook in all subjects dealing with issues related to enterprise management, including risk management. The methodology and conclusions presented herein can also be an inspiration in the process of writing diploma theses or industry analysis. The book complements and deepens the knowledge and research results in a very important business area, which is its key scientific and didactic value.

Zabrze, Poland Izabela Jonek-Kowalska

management. Furthermore, this issue is important both from a theoretical and practical point of view. The advantage of the book is also the use of the results of research conducted on a large group of enterprises and the development of the author's universal model for assessing the effectiveness of enterprise risk managers.

Given the above, the distinguishing features of this book include:

1. Of the researchban in the assessment and determinants of enterprise risk management effectiveness.

[illegible]

[illegible]

[illegible]

Acknowledgments

This book is financed from statutory research of Department of Economics and Computer Science (Silesian University of Technology) No. 13/010/BK_21/0057.

Summary

This monograph focuses on issues related to the effectiveness of risk management and the factors that determine this effectiveness in business practice. In the course of the conducted considerations and research, an answer was sought to the following research problem: *What factors affect the effectiveness of risk management and how can they be prioritised?* Research in this area has not been conducted on a larger scale before and its conduct has made it possible to fill the existing theoretical and practical gap in this area.

On the basis of literature studies and the analysis of the research results conducted so far in the area of risk management in the enterprise, four groups of factors potentially affecting the effectiveness of the use of methods and tools to mitigate threats and losses have been distinguished. These factors are:

- behavioural—related to the decision maker's perception of risk and its attitudes towards risk;
- methodical—related to the type and scope of the instruments used to manage the risk;
- resource—relating to the human, organisational and financial potential involved in the risk management process in the enterprise;
- environmental—related to the dangers in the immediate and distant environment of the enterprise.

In light of the research results obtained on a representative group of 722 Polish medium and large-sized enterprises it can be concluded that the most important group of factors influencing risk management effectiveness is the group of methodological factors. Resource factors also have a direct impact on the scale and scope of risk mitigation. In turn, behavioural factors influence decisions regarding the choice of risk management methods and tools. Therefore, they have an indirect impact on the effectiveness of risk management. In the course of the research, no statistically significant influence of environmental factors on risk management was found, which is most likely related to the inability of enterprises to influence the conditions of the immediate and distant environment.

The obtained research results allow us to better understand the attitudes of enterprises towards risk and also their decisions regarding the mitigation of threats and losses. They also make it possible to recognise the essence of risk management effectiveness and the factors that influence it. In turn, this can be used in theory and practice to design measures to improve risk management in enterprises.

Among the limitations of the conducted research, a research sample should be mentioned which included Polish large and medium-sized enterprises and thus was characterised by the national economic specificity. However, it is worth adding that the sample was selected in a random and representative manner which entitles us to generalise the research results on the population of large and medium-sized enterprises in Poland. Moreover, the risk management process itself including risk and loss mitigation instruments is universal and is used by all entities operating on a free market basis, therefore the obtained results and recommendations can be used in a wider scope than just Polish.

The opinion of the author of this monograph is that further directions of research on the effectiveness of risk management should include:

- comparative analyses carried out in other economic conditions;
- assessing the impact of the Covid-19 pandemic on corporate risk management and its effectiveness;

- confronting the results of qualitative research (conducted in this study) with the results of quantitative research taking into account the financial results of the surveyed enterprises;
- assessing the effectiveness of risk management in enterprises carried out on the basis of the ratio of expenditure incurred on mitigation of threats and losses to benefits obtained in connection with the actions taken in this regard.

Contents

List of Figures

List of Tables

1

Determinants of Risk Management Effectiveness: Previous Research and Conclusions

1.1 Fundamentals of Risk Management in an Enterprise

A characteristic feature of any human activity, including business, is the inability to predict the future and, consequently, the effects of decisions taken at the moment. In practice, this means a potential occurrence of previously unexpected decision consequences of a very diverse nature. This is related to the occurrence of uncertainty and associated risk.

The uncertainty results from the already mentioned inability to predict the future and from the complexity of the internal and external conditions of the functioning of any enterprise (De Vincentiis et al., 2019). Interestingly, in modern globalized and internationalized economies (Sengupta & Fanchon, 2009; Hoogvelt et al., 1987), the scale of uncertainty is increasing. Its range is also expanding by the increasing frequency and diversity of phenomena occurring incidentally in the past and treated as extraordinary events, such as natural disasters (fires, floods, tsunamis, earthquakes, etc.) and massive outbreaks of previously unknown diseases, as exemplified by the Covid-19 virus pandemic (Mishra, 2020; Karwot & Ober, 2019).

I. Jonek-Kowalska, *Effectiveness of Enterprise Risk Management*,
https://doi.org/10.1007/978-3-030-95376-8_1

Risk is the part of uncertainty from which it is distinguished by the ability to make predictions based on past data and information. In the case of risk, based on past observations and experiences, the company gains the opportunity to identify sources of potential risk. The company also has the ability to estimate the consequences of that risk (Krupa, 2002; Jajuga, 2018). This makes risk measurable (quantitatively or qualitatively), which fundamentally distinguishes it from unmeasurable and indeterminate uncertainty. Nevertheless, it is important to emphasize that the ability to estimate or measure risk is not the same as the ability to predict the future, but only means the chance to reduce the area of potential outcomes and consequences of decisions made.

In management, the precursors of research on uncertainty and risk were F.H. Knight and A.H. Willet, who defined both concepts and began research that gave rise to a new scientific paradigm now known as risk management (Michalski, 2008). Within this paradigm, quite a bit of space has been devoted to the discussion of the consequences of risk. This is because it can be assumed that the unforeseen consequences of risk occurrence are not only threats and their associated losses, but also opportunities and their associated gains. An advocate of such a perception of risk was P. Drucker (2006, 2016), who believed that an entrepreneur, when taking a risk, does not focus on avoiding threats, but primarily on seeking opportunities. This argumentation is also supported by the Old Italian root of the word risk associated with "courage" and "daring." Adherents of positive interpretation of risk form offensive trend in management (Sierpińska & Jachna, 2004), while their adversaries, preferring negative definition of risk are associated within defensive trend (Karmańska, 2008). An overview of the risk definitions in both trends is included in Table 1.1.

This monograph assumes, mainly due to the prevalence and practicality of the defensive trend, that risk is derived from uncertainty and associated with the possibility of negative deviation of the actual results of decisions from those originally planned. In this view, risk means the presence of unpredictable threats to the final outcome of a decision, as illustrated schematically in Fig. 1.1.

There are many different classifications of risk in the literature and in business practice. Given the nature and plan of the considerations carried

Table 1.1 Review of positive and negative risk definitions

Authors	Definition
Positive	
H. Braun	Risk is the possibility of both a negative and a positive deviation from the assumed target (Jędralska, 1992).
T. T. Kaczmarek	The possibility of failure, and in particular the possibility of the occurrence of events beyond the control of the acting subject, which they cannot accurately predict and cannot fully prevent, and which—by reducing utility results and / or by increasing expenditures—take the action either completely or partially away from the characteristics of effectiveness, benefit or economy.
C.A. Williams Jr., P.C. Young	Risk arises wherever activity creates potential gains or losses that cannot be predicted (Williams et al., 2002).
Negative	
B. Brühwiler	Danger of negative deviation from the target (Brühwiler, 1980).
E.J. Vaughen, T. Vaughen	A state of reality in which an undesirable event may occur, which is an unfavourable deviation (deviation from the expected result) (Vaughen & Vaughen, 1999).
J. Monkiewicz	An event that results in certain losses (Monkiewicz, 2000).
M. Sierpińska	Danger of failure to achieve the established goal while making a specific decision (Sierpińska & Jachna, 2004).

Source: Own work based on literature referenced in the Table 1.1

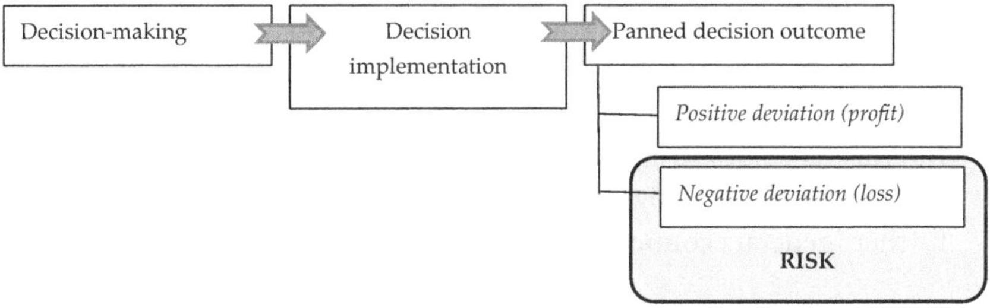

Fig. 1.1 Risk in the decision process. (Source: Own work)

out in this chapter, a decision was made to present those that will be used later in the monograph to build a model for assessing the effectiveness of risk management in the enterprise. Thus, the first of them refers to the type of activity carried out by the company and is reflected in the organizational structure of the company and in its documentation, including financial reporting.

In this context, the following risks can be distinguished:

- Operational, accompanying current activities undertaken in the enterprise of short-term scope (usually up to 1 year) (Zawiła-Niedźwiecki, 2009; Moosa, 2007); it concerns the issue "how resources are used in the organisational cycle to achieve the objective" (Zawiła-Niedźwiecki, 2014); according to Zawiła-Niedźwiecki (2014, p. 47) "operational risk is the risk of material and reputational loss and legal liability resulting from inadequate or failed processes and their essential resources (personnel, material, IT and financial), and the disruption emerging as a result of the impact of internal and external threats";
- Strategic, connected with investment and development activities with a long-term time horizon (more than a year); it concerns development plans, including the definition of development directions in the strategy (Urbanowska-Sojkin, 2013);
- Financial, related to the acquisition and use of own and debt capital and the account of economic profitability of operational and strategic activities; it accompanies both operational and strategic decisions involving financial resources (Michalak, 2016).

Considering the volatility of today's socioeconomic environment, an important classification of risk is also a division that includes risk (Islam & Tedford, 2012):

- Internal, accompanying resources and processes in the company;
- External, generated by the company's closer (market, industry) and further (general economic and international) environment.

The aforementioned risks are not separate but intertwined sets, which may lead to their mutual association and strengthen their impact on the company's performance. At the same time, the multitude and diversity of possible interconnections additionally complicate the estimation of probabilities and consequences of occurrence of specific risks.

Given the previous considerations, risk—regardless of its perception and type—means the possibility of threats to the implementation of the company's plans, which is why in the literature and practice there are efforts to counteract risks referred to as risk management (Tekathen & Dechow, 2013; Czajkowska, 2017; Kalinowski, 2007).

The main objectives of risk management can be viewed from two perspectives. The first relates to the prevention of threats that are the source of risk. The second includes actions oriented towards minimizing damage (losses) associated with the occurrence of given hazards (Łuczak, 2003). These objectives differ by the moment of intervention, as illustrated in Fig. 1.2.

In the case of prevention, risk management activities can be undertaken at the stage of identifying and assessing potential risks. In the case of prevention, risk management activities can be undertaken during the identification and assessment of potential hazards, while the planning and implementation of damage minimization activities are aimed at reducing the consequences of a risk occurring if it cannot be prevented. An example that illustrates both goals is the installation of fire extinguishers in a building (prevention) and cutting off fire-occupied areas from other premises/buildings (damage minimization) in the event of a fire. Of course, in the process of risk management, both goals should be achieved together, as this makes it possible to increase the effectiveness of protection against hazards.

Risk management is therefore a structured process aimed at preventing potential hazards and minimizing damage (loss) in the event of their occurrence (Soin & Collier, 2013; Kaczmarek, 2006). This process consists of four essential steps (Brustbauer, 2016):

1. Threats (risk) identification;
2. Risk assessment;

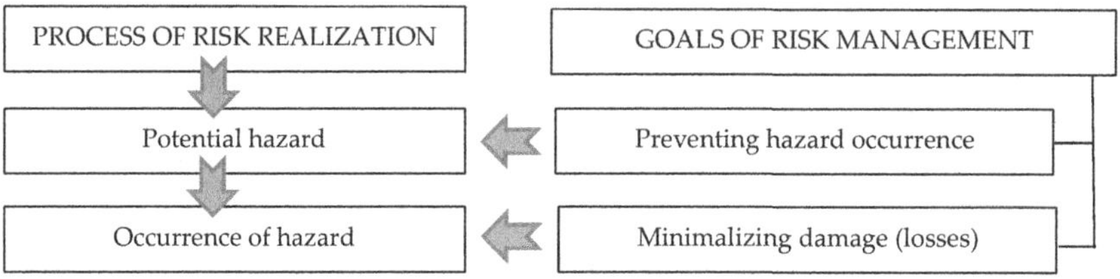

Fig. 1.2 Goals of enterprise risk management. (Source: Own work based on (Łuczak, 2003))

3. Risk mitigation;
4. Risk monitoring and control.

Threats identification involves the development of a so-called checklist containing all potential threats to the business. They should be characterized and systematized according to the accepted risk classification.

The list of risk sources should take into account the maximum number of threats, as it is the starting point for further stages of management (Czajkowska, 2017). Therefore, omission of significant risks will mean lack of action to mitigate them, which may have disastrous consequences for the company. For these reasons, it is advisable to conduct threats identification with the involvement of employees and external experts, which will allow taking into account different cognitive perspectives.

Risk assessment, which is the next stage of risk management, allows the following questions to be answered:

- What is the probability that a given source of risk (hazard) will occur?
- What damage (loss) can be caused by the occurrence of a given source of risk (hazard)?

This in turn allows each hazard to be assessed along two dimensions: probability—loss, and provides a starting point for classifying individual hazards according to the conceptual thinking illustrated in Fig. 1.3.

The classification shown in Fig. 1.3 identifies the sources of risk that pose the greatest threat to the business, i.e., those events that have the highest probability of occurrence and the highest level of loss if the risk is realized. It is on these that managers' attention should be focused in risk mitigation.

There are many risk assessment methods (Williams et al., 2002). Some of them are based on numerical data and take the form of quantitative methods using techniques typical of mathematics, statistics and econometrics. Some are qualitative and based on expert categorization of risk grading its intensity on a scale of small, medium and large (Bartusik & Cabała, 1997; Nahotko, 2001). None of the methods provides certainty as to the accuracy of the assessment, however, this is not a premise for

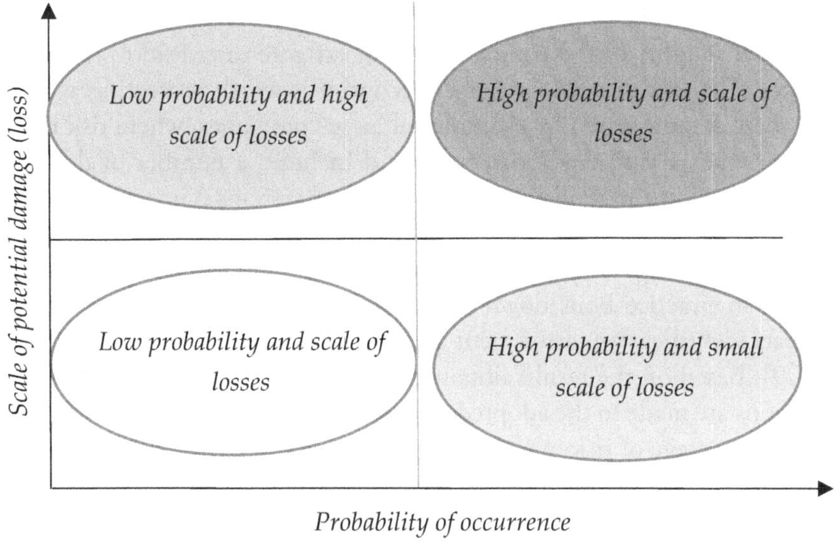

Fig. 1.3 Classification of sources of risk, taking into account the probability of occurrence and scale of potential damage (loss). (Source: Own work based on (Staniec & Klimczak, 2008; Mauermann & Oktem, 2002))

abandoning any form of risk validation, as even "flawed" methods provide better protection than their absence.

Risk mitigation—which is the next stage of risk management—consists of the selection and implementation of methods and tools that allow—in accordance with the objectives of risk management—to prevent the occurrence of a given threat or minimize the consequences of its occurrence. These methods and tools are adapted to the type of risk source identified and assessed. There are many of them in practice and theory. They are characterized by varying degrees of complexity and specificity. Among the most common ways of risk reduction, we can point to business insurance and regulations and procedures relating to occupational health and safety, which are found in virtually every business entity.

Notably, the implementation of risk mitigation methods and tools requires additional resource and financial expenditures. It is also time-consuming. The above circumstances often lead to ignoring risks or downplaying their effects (Chorafas, 2004).

Meanwhile, the implementation of many risks can seriously affect the financial stability of the company, and in extreme cases lead to its bankruptcy. The fact that risk is dangerous and it is worth protecting against it is best demonstrated by examples of large companies, where risk mitigation takes a very developed form and includes a number of detailed procedures forming holistic risk management systems (Gregoriou, 2007; Gorrod, 2004).

The final stage of risk management is its monitoring and control, which in practice boils down to ongoing observation of the effects of threats identification, assessment and mitigation (Chandra & Calderon, 2009). Based on the results obtained, adjustments, additions and modifications are made to the adopted risk management approaches. This is an important stage of risk management, although often overlooked in practice. It is worth noting that one-time implementation of risk management methods and tools does not guarantee their continuous relevance and effectiveness. Risks change over time, both in terms of frequency, type and intensity of occurrence. The extent of a company's exposure to risk, and thus the scale of possible damage and losses, changes with it. Hence monitoring and control should be a permanent, recurring component of risk management in any enterprise.

1.2 Efficiency and Effectiveness of Enterprise Risk Management

Agility, efficiency and effectiveness are key parameters for assessing the results of operational and strategic decisions. They can, therefore, also be applied to risk management, which is why in the following subsection these concepts are defined and adapted for the research presented in this monograph.

In general terms, agility is the ability of a company to undertake economic activities, which in practice means being equipped with the necessary tangible and intangible resources and having the ability to use them in production and service processes. It is a necessary condition for the survival and development of any organization (Zieleniewski, 1969; Krzakiewicz, 2006).

Effectiveness is associated with the ability to set rational goals and to "do the right things", i.e., to take actions aimed at achieving the specified operational and strategic intentions (Gilbert et al., 2011; Griffin, 2013). In this definitional context, evaluation and measurement of effectiveness take place by determining to what extent the company has achieved its planned objectives. The higher the degree of goal achievement, the higher the effectiveness.

Efficiency, on the other hand, allows evaluating the ratio of effects to the expenses incurred to achieve the company's goals (Skrzypek, 2012). The combination of effectiveness and efficiency evaluation is very important, because high efficiency does not always mean high effectiveness. This is because a situation may occur in which objectives are achieved efficiently and effectively, but at very high expenditures, inadequate to the achieved results. Then the company is exposed to losses, the accumulation of which may, in extreme cases, lead to its bankruptcy.

Measurable evaluation of efficiency in practice is carried out by means of specific indicators, adapted to the circumstances of measurement and reflecting the defining relation of effects to inputs (Ng, 2009). The most popular measures of efficiency are profitability ratios used to assess economic efficiency, and efficiency and productivity ratios used to assess the results of human labor and technical infrastructure, respectively (Sengupta & Sahoo, 2006; Wu, 2008).

Given that the objective of risk management is to prevent risks and minimize damage and loss, both the effectiveness and efficiency of the process should be assessed in this context. Therefore, the **effectiveness of risk management** is the degree to which the company is protected against internal and external risks as a result of the activities undertaken as part of the process (threats identification, assessment, mitigation and monitoring and control).

The assessment of risk management effectiveness can be undertaken in relation to individual risks, or it can relate to the functioning of the company as a whole, which can be particularly useful if the company uses a holistic risk management system (Jonek-Kowalska, 2019). This assessment should be a permanent part of risk management monitoring and control (Trzeciak & Jonek-Kowalska, 2021), as its results allow answering the question of, *Have the enterprise's risk management methods and techniques protected it from risks, and to what extent?* If the answer to this question with respect to individual strategic and operational activities is not satisfactory, it is a signal to implement corrective actions and improve the enterprise's risk management procedures, so that the mere fact of implementing these procedures does not constitute sufficient and sole evidence of the existence of protection against threats.

Assessing the effectiveness of risk management is also important in the context of the potential for overregulation of the process. In many companies, particularly large ones, there are highly elaborate and bureaucratic risk management procedures that constitute an additional, not necessarily desirable, obligation for employees, often carried out mechanically and without thinking. Notably, managers often recognize the existence of risk *post factum*, that is, after it has materialized. Assessing effectiveness can keep them alert and ready. Just how important such attitudes are is evidenced by the lack of preparedness for the Covid-19 pandemic crisis resulting largely from a passive or even dismissive attitude to risk.

An important, albeit much more difficult, issue in enterprise risk management is the **assessment of effectiveness**. This effectiveness, according to the earlier definition, is expressed by the ratio of the effects of risk mitigation expressed as the degree of minimization (avoidance) of losses to the expenses incurred for risk management, which, in general form, is expressed by the following formula:

$$RM_{ef} = \frac{results\ of\ risk\ mitigation\left(limiting\ losses\right)}{expenditure\ on\ risk\ mitigation} \tag{1.1}$$

where:

RM_{ef}—means the static, short-term risk management effectiveness.

It defines effectiveness in absolute (percentage) terms, which creates a basis for comparison between individual processes and companies. It is also easy to interpret and allows setting desirable limits of profitability of risk management. If the value of the indicator exceeds 1.0 (100%) then the process is profitable because the result is higher than the effort undertaken to achieve it. If the value of the indicator is less than 1.0 (100%) then risk management does not bring the desired results because the company spends more on mitigation than the reduction of potential losses achieved through this expenditure. The interpretation of Formula 1.1 is also clear, according to which the effectiveness of risk management in a company increases as the value of the indicator increases.

Taking into account the fact that risk management is a continuous process and therefore long-term, the assessment of its effectiveness can be approached similarly to the assessment of the profitability of investment projects and its measurement can be performed using the Net Present Value (*NPV*)) formula transformed to the following form:

$$NRM_{ef} = \sum_{t=0}^{n} \frac{R_{RMt} - O_{RMt}}{(1+d)^{t}} \tag{1.2}$$

where:

NRM_{ef}—means the dynamic, long-term risk management effectiveness;
R_{RMt}—results of risk management in subsequent periods (t);
O_{RMt}—expenditures on risk management in subsequent periods (t);
t—subsequent periods (t);
d—the discount rate reflecting the change in the time value of money.

Formula 1.2 makes it possible not only to measure performance over the long term, but also to set standards in risk management performance. If it is negative, NRM_{ef} risk management will be unprofitable because the expenses incurred in the process will exceed the benefits in terms of avoiding potential losses. The risk management profitability conditions can therefore be written as the following relationships:

$$NRM_{ef} < 0 - risk\ management\ is\ unprofitable \tag{1.3}$$

$$NRM_{ef} \geq 0 - risk\ management\ is\ profitable \tag{1.4}$$

As with assessing effectiveness, evaluating the effectiveness of risk management can apply to individual actions, such as hedging against currency risk through the use of derivatives, or it can relate to the entire enterprise, but in this case, it will require identifying and adding up all the inputs and outputs of risk management. A catalog of examples of inputs to enterprise risk management is shown in Table 1.2.

Estimating inputs for risk mitigation—like estimating inputs in a traditional investment project—requires a certain degree of care and accuracy, but can be carried out without major methodological problems (Howell, 2020) in contrast to assessing the results of risk management. This assessment is hampered by the mere potential reduction in damages and risks achieved by risk mitigation and the fact that it deals with future periods and events whose existence the company cannot foresee. As a result, the assessment of risk management results is an estimate and is a subject to significant computational error. This error can be minimized by developing variant scenarios for calculating the results of risk mitigation (optimistic, pessimistic, realistic) similarly to the already mentioned traditional investment projects.

Table 1.2 Examples of expenditures associated with enterprise risk management from a resource perspective

Resources involved in risk management	Financial dimension of the effort involved in risk management
Human	Remuneration of employees involved in risk management; Expenditure on external risk management consultancy and reports;
Material	Costs of securing (prevention) the company's assets against risks associated with: fire protection, compliance with health and safety regulations, prevention of extraordinary events (flood, inundation, hurricane, earthquake, etc.);
Financial	Costs of property and personal insurance (premiums, insurance fees and commissions) related to physical and human resources; Costs of protecting against financial risk (currency risk, credit risk, loss of liquidity risk, bankruptcy risk) related to the resources and financial situation of the company, e.g., costs of using derivative instruments, financial insurance (credit risk, loss of profit risk, etc.).

Source: Own work

It is worth noting, however, that regardless of the adopted methodology for assessing the effectiveness and efficiency of risk management in the process of monitoring and controlling risks, it is necessary to ask whether the adopted methods and tools to protect the company against threats bring the desired results and what expenses the company incurs in connection with this protection.

The remainder of this monograph focuses on identifying the determinants of risk management effectiveness by adopting the definitional assumptions presented in this subsection and seeking answers to the question of what makes risk mitigation meet the expectations placed in it.

1.3 Systematization of Determinants of Effectiveness and Efficiency of Enterprise Risk Management

As already mentioned, there is a great deal of literature on the stages and methods of risk management and as indicated by Fraser et al. (2021) this is still a topic of current interest for managers. It also raises questions about methods for assessing the effectiveness of risk management systems. Practitioners indicate that they make such an assessment using most often the methodology of internal audit. Based on its results, they also decide on possible improvements and additions to the existing solutions (Fraser et al., 2021).

The scientific and research assessment of the effectiveness of risk management in an enterprise is very strongly influenced by the dynamics of changes in the socio-economic environment, on which the scope and intensity of risk depends. Thus, due to the increasing level of climatic and pandemic risks (Jaziri & Miralam, 2021; Baz & Ruel, 2021), the subject of disasters and the use of risk management in emergency situations has received considerable attention in the literature in recent years (Chen et al., 2021; Fernandez, 2021; Räsänen, 2021). Consequently, there is a growing body of research focused on linking risk management with shaping the resilience of different organizations to threats and crises. This is to go beyond the existing patterns of risk management and complement them with a broader context related to the need to adapt to the increasingly turbulent and complex socio-economic environment (Soufi et al., 2021).

A new challenge associated with the increasing digitization of economies and societies is also the maintenance of cyber security and the prevention of IT threats. This issue is receiving a great deal of attention in economic theory and practice (Lee, 2021; Żywiołek, 2018). It is particularly relevant in the financial sector, where customer capitals are exposed to cyber-attacks (Varga et al., 2021).

It is also worth noting that the abundance of publications on risk management appearing in recent years—a direct result of the increased volatility of the environment—clearly highlights the importance of these issues and the impact of risk management in increasing the effectiveness of protection against growing internal and external threats.

As signaled, risk management is a formalized process that operates according to clarified rules. Research shows that such an arrangement and the integration of risk management into the organizational structure of an enterprise promotes improved security and increases the effectiveness of risk management (Tagod et al., 2021). It is also important to integrate the different stages of risk management and the knowledge used in the threats identyfication and assessment process (Okudan et al., 2021). Indeed, research suggests that a systems approach to risk management increases its effectiveness (Miao et al., 2021). Furthermore, it contributes to a more accurate calculation of the inputs and benefits of risk management (Langdalen et al., 2020).

In the methodological context of risk management, comparisons of the effectiveness of threats identification and evaluation methods are also conducted. These studies conclude that holistic risk evaluation tools that cover the entire enterprise's operations produce better results than single methods tailored to assess specific risks (Fu et al., 2020; Sharan & Narayanan, 2020). They can also improve the degree of financial health measured as the distance to default (González et al., 2020).

Researchers also highlight the role of human resources in risk management, as managers make decisions about the rules and ways to mitigate risks, and employees implement them. Their impact on effectiveness is therefore direct and significant. As Jia and Bradbury (2020) highlight, the competence and independence of risk management teams and the quality of human resources play a significant role in effectively protecting financial performance from risk exposure. An important stimulant of risk effectiveness is also the awareness and inclusion of employees in the risk management system, so that procedures and resources are fully integrated (Kirin et al., 2021).

It is also worth noting that, from an entity perspective, risk management is most often used—studied and described—in large and medium-sized enterprises. The SME sector is very neglected in this respect and, consequently, is also poorly protected against risks (Marcelino-Sadaba & Perez-Ezcurdia, 2010; Alquier & Tignol, 2006). On an industry basis, those sectors where the intensity of hazards is very intense and/or atypical are most often analyzed. These include, but are not limited to, mining (Fa & Li, 2021; Tubis et al., 2020), construction, chemicals, and the aforementioned information technology (Filippetto et al., 2021) and financial (Nazaire et al., 2020) industries.

As the previous discussion shows, the effectiveness of risk management depends on the following determinants:

- The intensity and frequency of endo- and exogenous risks, the more numerous and more frequent they are, the more difficult they are to mitigate, which may negatively affect the ultimate effectiveness of risk management;
- The choice and principles of using methods and tools for risk management in the enterprise, the more relevant and better adapted to the needs of the enterprise, the greater the chance for effective protection against threats and their consequences;
- The characteristics, attitudes and behaviors of managers and employees (human resources) in the process of implementation and application of risk management principles, which can be a stimulant or destimulant of effectiveness depending on their individual arrangement described in more detail later in this publication.

The aforementioned groups of determinants apply to: Risk genesis (internal and external threats), risk management methodology and resource factor. In such a system they will be characterized in the following chapters, and then will be used to develop a model for assessing the effectiveness of risk management in the enterprise. It should also be added that the effectiveness of risk management will be evaluated primarily in the context of the triad: risk—security—continuity (Zawiła-Niedźwiecki, 2003, 2010, 2014). This is because risk management is designed to protect the enterprise from threats in order to ensure its interruption in the short term and development in the long term. In practice, this means that operational risk management should protect the company's current financial performance, while strategic risk management should focus on enhancing value for all stakeholders.

References

Alquier, A. M. B., & Tignol, M. H. L. (2006). Risk management in small- and medium-sized enterprises. *Production Planning & Control, 17*(3), 273–282.

Bartusik, K., & Cabała, K. (1997). Metoda scenariuszy w planowaniu strategicznym. *Przegląd Organizacji, 2*, 23–29.

Baz, J. E., & Ruel, S. (2021). Can supply chain risk management practices mitigate the disruption impacts on supply chains' resilience and robustness? Evidence from an empirical survey in a COVID-19 outbreak era. *International Journal of Production Economics, 233*, 107972.

Brühwiler, B. (1980). *Risk management—eine Aufgabe der Unternehmensführung* (p. 40). Verlag Paul Haubt.

Brustbauer, J. (2016). Enterprise risk management in SMEs: Towards a structural model. *International Small Business Journal, 34*(1), 70–85.

Chandra, A., & Calderon, T. H. (2009). Information intensity, control deficiency risk, and materiality. *Managerial Auditing Journal, 4*(3), 18–24.

Chen, X., Chong, W. F., Feng, R., & Zhang, L. (2021). Pandemic risk management: Resources contingency planning and allocation Xiaowei Chen, Wing Fung Chong, Runhuan Feng, Linfeng Zhang Insurance: Mathematics and Economics, vol. 101, pp. 359–383. *Insurance: Mathematics and Economics.* Available online 17 August 2021. In press.

Chorafas, D. (2004). *Risk management. The bottleneck is at the top of the bottle.* Palgrave Macmillan UK.

Czajkowska, K. (2017). Metody identyfikacji ryzyka w zarządzaniu ryzykiem w przedsiębiorstwie. *Journal of Modern Management Process, 2*(1), 40–49.
De Vincentiis, P., Culasso, F., & Cerrato, S. A. (Eds.). (2019). *The future of risk management.* Palgrave Macmillan UK.
Drucker, P. F. (2006). *The effective executive.* HarperCollins Publishers.
Drucker, P. F. (2016). *Managing the non-profit organization. Principles and practice.* Routledge.
Fa, Z., & Li, X. (2021). From aggregate to part: Study on the change of coal mine safety records in China under the intervention of risk pre-control management system. *Resources Policy, 73*, 102159.
Fernandez, M. (2021). Risk perceptions and management strategies in a post-disaster landscape of Guatemala: Social conflict as an opportunity to understand disaster. *International Journal of Disaster Risk Reduction, 57*, 10153.
Filippetto, A. S., Lima, R., & Barbosa, J. L. V. (2021). A risk prediction model for software project management based on similarity analysis of context histories. *Information and Software Technology, 131*, 106497.
Fraser, J. R. S., Qualil, R., & Simkins, J. (2021). Questions that are asked about enterprise risk management by risk practitioners. *Business Horizons.* In press.
Fu, Y., Sun, Q., & Wennersten, R. (2020). Effectiveness of the CVaR method in risk management in an integrated energy system. *Energy Reports, 6*(9), 1010–1015.
Gilbert, D. R., Stoner, J. A. F., & Freeman, E. R. (2011). *Kierowanie.* Wydawnictwo Naukowe PWN.
González, L. O., Santomil, P. D., & Herrera, A. T. (2020). The effect of Enterprise Risk Management on the risk and the performance of Spanish listed companies. *European Research on Management and Business Economics, 26*(3), 111–120.
Gorrod, M. (2004). *Risk management systems. Process, technology and trends.* Palgrave Macmillan UK.
Gregoriou, G. (Ed.). (2007). *Advances in risk management.* Palgrave Macmillan UK.
Griffin, R. W. (2013). *Podstawy zarządzania organizacjami.* Wydawnictwo Naukowe PWN.
Hoogvelt, A., Puxty, A. G., Buckley, P. J., & Omarov, Y. (1987). *Multinational enterprise. An encyclopedic dictionary of concepts and terms.* Palgrave Macmillan UK.
Howell, S. T. (2020). Firm type variation in the cost of risk management. *Journal of Corporate Finance, 64*, 101691.

Islam, A., & Tedford, D. (2012). Risk determinants of small and medium-sized manufacturing enterprises (SMEs)—An exploratory study in New Zealand. *Journal of Industrial Engineering International, 8*(1), 8–15.
Jajuga, K. (2018). *Zarządzanie ryzykiem.* Wydawnictwo Naukowe PWN.
Jaziri, R., & Miralam, M. S. (2021). The impact of crisis and disasters risk management in COVID-19 times: Insights and lessons learned from Saudi Arabia. *Ethics, Medicine and Public Health, 18*, 100705.
Jędralska, K. (1992). *Zachowania przedsiębiorstw w sytuacjach niepewnych i ryzykownych* (p. 49). Wydawnictwo Akademii Ekonomicznej w Katowicach.
Jia, J., & Bradbury, M. E. (2020). Complying with best practice risk management committee guidance and performance. *Journal of Contemporary Accounting & Economics, 16*(3), 100225.
Jonek-Kowalska, I. (2019). Efficiency of Enterprise Risk Management (ERM) systems. Comparative analysis in the fuel sector and energy sector on the basis of Central-European companies listed on the Warsaw Stock Exchange. *Resources Policy, 62*, 415–425.
Kaczmarek, T. T. (2006). *Ryzyko i zarządzanie ryzykiem. Ujęcie interdyscyplinarne*. Difin.
Kalinowski, M. (2007). *Zarządzanie ryzykiem walutowym w przedsiębiorstwie*. CeDeWu.
Karmańska, A. (2008). Neoklasyczne ramy analizy atrybutów ryzyka. In A. Karmańska (Ed.), *Ryzyko w rachunkowości*. Difin.
Karwot, J., & Ober, J. (2019). Safety management of water economy. Case study of the water and sewerage company. *Management Systems in Production Engineering, 3*, 189–196.
Kirin, S., Sedmak, A., Lic, W., Brzaković, M., Miljanoviće, I., Petrović, A., & Sedmaka, S. (2021). Human factor risk management procedures applied in the case of open pit mine. *Engineering Failure Analysis, 126*, 105456.
Krupa, M. (2002). *Ryzyko i niepewność w zarządzaniu*. Antykwa.
Krzakiewicz, K. (2006). *Teoretyczne podstawy organizacji i zarządzania*. Wydawnictwo Akademii Ekonomicznej w Poznaniu.
Langdalen, H., Abrahamsen, E. B., & Selvik, J. T. (2020). On the importance of systems thinking when using the ALARP principle for risk management. *Reliability Engineering & System Safety, 204*, 107222.
Lee, I. (2021). Cybersecurity: Risk management framework and investment cost analysis. *Business Horizons, 64*(5), 659–671.
Łuczak, M. (2003). *Ryzyko i kryzys w zarządzaniu przedsiębiorstwem*. Wyższa Szkoła Ekonomiczna.

Marcelino-Sadaba, S., & Perez-Ezcurdia, A. (2010). Risk management in SME's tackled projects. *Dyna, 85*(6), 504–512.
Mauermann, A., & Oktem, U. (2002). The near-miss management in operational risk. *The Journal of Risk Finance, 4*(1), 25–38.
Miao, D., Yu, K., Zhou, L., Jin, W., & Chen, H. (2021). Dynamic risks hierarchical management and control technology of coal chemical enterprises. *Journal of Loss Prevention in the Process Industries, 71*, 104466.
Michalak, A. (2016). The cost of capital in the effectiveness assessment of financial management in a company. *Oeconomia Copernicana, 7*(2), 317–332.
Michalski, T. (2008). *Filozoficzne i klasyczne podstawy definiowania ryzyka*. In A. Karmańska (Ed.), *Ryzyko w rachunkowości*. Difin.
Mishra, P. K. (2020). COVID-19, Black Swan events and the future of disaster risk management in India. *Progress in Disaster Science, 8*, 100137.
Monkiewicz, J. (2000). *Podstawy ubezpieczeń* (p. 16). Poltext.
Moosa, I. (2007). *Operational risk management*. Palgrave Macmillan UK.
Nahotko, S. (2001). *Ryzyko ekonomiczne w działalności gospodarczej*. Oficyna Wydawnicza Ośrodka Postępu Organizacyjnego Spółka z o.o.
Nazaire, G., Pacurar, M., & Sy, O. (2020). Factor investing and risk management: Is smart-beta diversification smart? *Finance Research Letters, 41*, 101854.
Ng, Y. (2009). *Increasing returns and economic efficiency*. Palgrave Macmillan UK.
Okudan, O., Budayan, C., & Dikmen, I. (2021). A knowledge-based risk management tool for construction projects using case-based reasoning. *Expert Systems with Applications, 173*, 114776.
Räsänen, A. (2021). Cross-scale interactions in flood risk management: A case study from Rovaniemi, Finland. *International Journal of Disaster Risk Reduction, 57*, 10185.
Sengupta, J. K., & Fanchon, P. (2009). *Efficiency, market dynamics and industry growth*. Palgrave Macmillan UK.
Sengupta, J. K., & Sahoo, B. (2006). *Efficiency models in data envelopment analysis. Techniques of evaluation of productivity of firms in a growing economy*. Palgrave Macmillan UK.
Sharan, K., & Narayanan, K. R. M. (2020). Review on construction risk and development of risk management procedural index—A case study from Chennai construction sector. *Materials Today: Proceedings, 29*, 1141–1146.
Sierpińska, M., & Jachna, T. (2004). *Ocena przedsiębiorstwa według standardów światowych*. Wydawnictwo Naukowe PWN.
Skrzypek, E. (2012). *Efektywność ekonomiczna jako ważny czynnik sukcesu organizacji*. Prace Naukowe Uniwersytetu Ekonomicznego we Wrocławiu, 262.

Soin, K., & Collier, P. (2013). Risk and risk management in management accounting and control. *Management Accounting Research, 24*, 82–87.
Soufi, H. R., Esfahanipour, A., & Shirazi, M. A. (2021). Risk reduction through enhancing risk management by resilience. *International Journal of Disaster Risk Reduction, 64*, 102497.
Staniec, J., & Klimczak, K. M. (2008). *Zarządzanie ryzykiem operacyjnym*. Wydawnictwo C.H. Beck.
Tagod, M., Adeleke, A. Q., & Moshood, T. D. (2021). Coercive pressure as a moderator of organizational structure and risk management: Empirical evidence from Malaysian construction industry. *Journal of Safety Research, 77*, 1390150.
Tekathen, M., & Dechow, N. (2013). Enterprise risk management and continuous re-alignment in the pursuit of accountability: A German case. *Management Accounting Research, 24*(2), 100–121.
Trzeciak, M., & Jonek-Kowalska, I. (2021). Monitoring and control in program management as effectiveness drivers in polish energy sector. Diagnosis and directions of improvement. *Energies, 14*(15), 4661.
Tubis, A., Werbínska-Wojciechowska, S., & Wroblewski, A. (2020). Risk assessment methods in mining industry—A systematic review. *Applied Science, 10*, 51168–55172.
Urbanowska-Sojkin, E. (2013). *Ryzyko w wyborach strategicznych w przedsiębiorstwach*. PWE.
Varga, S., Brynielsson, J., & Franke, U. (2021). Cyber-threat perception and risk management in the Swedish financial sector. *Computers & Security, 105*, 102239.
Vaughen, E. J., & Vaughen, T. (1999). *Fundamental of risk and insurance* (pp. 3–4). John Wiley & Sons.
Williams, C. A., Smith, M. L., & Young, P. C. (2002). *Zarządzanie ryzykiem a ubezpieczenia*. Wydawnictwo Naukowe PWN.
Wu, Y. (2008). *Productivity, efficiency and economic growth in China*. Palgrave Macmillan UK.
Zawiła-Niedźwiecki, J. (2003). *Metoda TSM-BCP—Total security management, business continuity planning*. European Network Security Institute.
Zawiła-Niedźwiecki, J. (2009). Operational risk and the security of an organization. In J. Monkiewicz & L. Gąsiorkiewicz (Eds.), *Risk management. Concepts, models, issues*. Dom Wydawniczy Elipsa.
Zawiła-Niedźwiecki, J. (2010). Business continuity. *Foundations of Management, 2*(2), 101–119.

Zawiła-Niedźwiecki, J. (2014). *Operational risk as a problematic triad: Risk—Resource security—Business continuity*. Edu-Libri.

Zieleniewski, J. (1969). *Organizacja i zarządzanie*. Wydawnictwo Naukowe PWN.

Żywiołek, J. (2018). Monitoring of information security system elements in the enterprise. *MATEC Web of Conferences*. https://doi.org/10.1051/matecconf/201818301007

2

Behavioral Determinants of Risk Management Effectiveness

2.1 Risk Perception: Opportunity or Threat?

It follows from the considerations presented in the first chapter that risk accompanies every decision, which means that its scale and intensity depends on the choices made by the decision-maker (manager). These, in turn, are strongly determined by a rather individual set of behavioral traits that each person is equipped with.

Previous research (Jędralska, 1992; Jonek-Kowalska & Wawiernia, 2016) shows that the way of responding to risk and risk mitigation is influenced by three main behavioral factors, which are:

- Risk perception,
- Propensity to take risks,
- Attitudes towards risk.

These factors will be described in detail in the following subsections and then incorporated into the adopted research model.

The first is perception (perceptions) defined as a cognitive process involving an individual's subjective reflection of objects, phenomena, and

I. Jonek-Kowalska, *Effectiveness of Enterprise Risk Management*,
https://doi.org/10.1007/978-3-030-95376-8_2

processes. It is a registration of elements of the external world including: their sensory reception, understanding, identification and verbal determination, and preparation for response to a stimulus (Jeziorska, 2013). Thus, the characteristic feature of perception is its close connection with the person of the decision maker and, consequently, significant individualization.

Risk perception is related to the described currents of defining this concept: offensive and defensive. In the former, risk is identified with an opportunity or threat, while in the latter it has only negative connotations and means a threat to the company's operations (Jajuga & Jajuga, 2006). The above dichotomy translates into the perception of risk by managers. For some, it is an attractive challenge and an opportunity to undertake entrepreneurial and innovative activities, while for others it represents only a danger causing damage and losses (Douglas, 2009; Ober, 2020).

Individual perception of risk is influenced by two factors. The first is the decision maker's general, life-long attitude resulting from his or her personality traits, referred to as affectivity (Isen & Baron, 1991). Affectivity to be positive or negative. If a manager is characterized by positive affectivity, then he/she usually perceives risk as an opportunity to be taken in order to realize the challenge and achieve the desired benefits and rewards. If the manager is characterized by negative affectivity, then the manager perceives risk as a threat that must be prevented in order to minimize damage and loss (Isen & Geva, 1988). Of course, the above characteristics represent the extremes of risk perception. In between, there are also more balanced visions of the effects of risk projecting into the final reactions and choices of the decision maker depending also on the circumstances of their making.

In addition to affectivity, risk perception is also influenced by what is known as experience history, which shapes the decision maker's past associations with the consequences of risk implementation. Thus, if a manager has realized gains more often in connection with risk-taking, he will view risk as an opportunity. If, on the other hand, risk is more often associated with losses, he will perceive it as a threat. At the same time, it is also worth noting that as time passes and experience history increases, managers show a greater tendency to equate risk with damage and threat, suggesting that the perception of risk is also affected by the age of the decision maker (Sołtysiak, 2014; Douglas, 2009). Nonetheless, it is worth adding that some studies indicate that recent memories matter most in the history of experiences, and decision makers are less likely to consider the totality of past experiences (Campara et al., 2021).

In addition to age, gender also influences risk perception. Research suggests that women, who are inherently more cautious, are more likely to associate risk with danger, damage, and loss (Sołtysiak, 2014; Ameljańczyk, 2017). When evaluating potential risks, they tend to assess them as more likely and more likely to result in losses than men. They also tend to overestimate risk (Brown et al., 2021).

It should be noted, however, that gender diversity in corporate boardrooms, and hence diversity in risk perception, may have a positive effect on risk protection (Brown et al., 2021; Cho et al., 2021; Mohsni et al., 2021; Qayyum et al., 2021; Zhu et al., 2021), which is most likely due to the balance of risk perception between the two genders favoring risk objectification. Studies also suggest that women are more willing to take risks the higher the accompanying benefits are (Abou-El-Sood, 2021), which means that they do not avoid risky decisions, but consider them worth taking in situations with more certainty and higher rewards.

In addition to the aforementioned factors, cognitive distortions signifying exaggerated and/or irrational thinking patterns also influence risk perception. Among those most relevant to risk management are (Macko & Tyszka, 2005):

- a manager's assessment of his or her own probability of failure as lower than that of others in the same situation;
- manager's assessment of certain events as less probable or less likely to cause losses, in a situation in which he/she has a direct influence on their course.

The above circumstances are referred to as unrealistic optimism (Wyrozębski et al., 2012), which has a very negative effect on the consequences of risk realization because it causes underestimation of risks, which consequently increases the probability and extent of damage and loss.

2.2 Propensity to Take Risks

Behavioral determinant of risk management effectiveness is also risk appetite, which means the level of willingness to engage in activities with uncertain, hardly predictable outcome (Tyszka & Domurat, 2004). It varies widely and, in simple terms, can be expressed by the following 3 statements:

- I like risk and am willing to take it.
- I am indifferent to risk and risk-taking activities.
- I do not like risk and I am reluctant to take it.

According to the above, decision makers with high risk propensity perceive risk but fear it to a lesser extent than those who dislike risk. In corporate operations, the risk propensity of managers is very important. Excessive risk appetite can be associated with bravado and overexposure of the enterprise to risk. In turn, aversion to risky activities may paralyze economic activity and hinder the company's growth. Then risk aversion—presented as prudence and caution—becomes an excuse for the incompetence and indecision of the decision maker.

Nevertheless, it should be clearly emphasized that in undertaking entrepreneurial and innovative activities, an above-average propensity to take risks is desirable and very valuable, since most people are characterized by risk aversion (Wieczorek, 2013). Meanwhile, running one's own business and performing management functions involves many risky decisions, which requires at least acceptance of risk. Previous research clearly shows that higher risk propensity is associated with higher entrepreneurship and innovation, without which progress and development of economies and societies would not be possible (Cui et al., 2016; Wang et al., 2016).

Risk propensity is influenced by individual patterns of coping with risky situations and the aforementioned history of experience. Risk propensity may change over time as the mentioned patterns and individual experience history change (Arena et al., 2010). It should also be added that it is also declarative and does not always coincide with actual attitudes towards risk realized in the decision-making process.

The gender of the decision-maker is also a determinant of risk appetite. Women are more likely than men to fear risk and less willing to take it, which undoubtedly stems from their threat perception of risk, characterized in the previous section. Men, more likely to perceive risk as an opportunity, are more likely to engage in decisions and actions with uncertain outcomes (Bajcar, 2012, 2017; Hysa & Rakowska, 2014).

Risk appetite is also influenced by the age of the decision maker, which is partly related to experience history. Younger managers unburdened by many failures and mistakes are more willing to accept risks accompanying individual decisions than their older colleagues equipped with a greater baggage of professional practice (Arena et al., 2010).

In addition to the above factors, individual personality variables also influence risk appetite, as shown in Table 2.1.

Apart from individual determinants such as age, gender and personality, environmental and situational factors also have an impact on the propensity to take risks. The former are related to cultural and national determinants. Previous research shows that the propensity to risk depends on the country of origin and the overall spiritual and material achievements of a given society (Czauderna, 2016; Majewska-Bielecka, 2012; Pilch & Rosmus, 2004; Tyszka & Domurat, 2004). Indeed, the culture of a society at the national level influences the system of values, attitudes, and the way emotions are expressed (Astakhova et al., 2017). A clear example of such influence is the impact of upbringing on risk-taking propensity and entrepreneurship in paternalistic and materialistic societies. As Shahriar (2018) shows, the dominant gender role in a given culture or society determines the frequency of men or women starting their own businesses. Due to the permanence and integrity of the indicated environmental factors with the decision maker/manager, they are difficult to shape and change in the short term.

Situational factors, on the other hand, are temporary in nature, dependent on the circumstances surrounding a given decision, making them changeable and context-dependent. Among them, the most commonly mentioned (Pilch & Rosmus, 2004) are:

Table 2.1 Individual, personality determinants of risk propensity

Group of determinants	Description of determinants
Motivational	These are factors related to: • individual aspirations and motivations set by the ceiling of personal and professional goals; • Behavioral patterns in case of failure in achieving personal and professional goals. Individuals with high aspirations, who are highly motivated and success-oriented and who cope well with failure show a higher propensity to take risks than individuals with lower aspirations, weaker motivation and who do not cope with failure.
Emotional	These are factors related to the emotions evoked by risk, which may be: • excitement • or fear. Individuals who feel excitement in situations fraught with uncertainty are more likely to take risks than individuals who feel anxiety/fear in such situations. Research also suggests that as a decision maker's self-control increases, their willingness to take risks decreases (Sekścińska et al., 2021).
Cognitive	These are factors pertaining to one's individual conception of how the world is perceived and described. They include elements such as the conceptual categories used, reflexivity and impulsivity, and the perception of one's own agency. Individuals with higher impulsivity and lower reflexivity who feel high self-efficacy are more likely to take risks than individuals who are less impulsive, reflexive, and subject to the causal power of other people/entities.

Source: Own study based on: (Wiśniewska-Szatek, 2005; Pilch & Rosmus, 2004)

- The amount of possible loss or reward.
- The likelihood of a particular outcome.
- Level of knowledge about the risk.
- The ability to control the situation.
- Emotions associated with the situation.

The influence of situational factors on the propensity to take risks in extreme cases can be significant and change the decision maker/manager's previous attitude towards risks (Pera, 2013). Examples of this can be herd behavior, change of decisions under the influence of coercion or strong emotions of different background accompanying the event. However, it is important to add that situational factors have only a transient effect on the propensity to take risks. Once the event-related circumstances cease, the previously formed long-term risk propensity remains largely unchanged (Cantarella et al., 2015).

2.3 Attitudes towards Risk

The last of the behavioral variables influencing the effectiveness of enterprise risk management are attitudes towards risk, which are at the same time the product of risk perception and risk appetite (Tavor, 2019; Jaramillo & Vargas, 2019; Nax & Newton, 2019).

Risk perception and risk propensity reflect certain integral characteristics of the decision maker and are generally associated with him over a long period of time (Zhang & Li, 2021). They determine how a person makes decisions and thus influence the type and extent of risk he or she will ultimately take. These relationships are schematically illustrated in Fig. 2.1.

Perceiving risk in a positive way (also as an opportunity) is most often associated with a preference for risky situations and more frequent risk-taking, which means an active attitude towards opportunities and threats, characteristic of entrepreneurs and innovators. Perceiving risk only as a threat is typical of decision makers who are averse to risky decisions and events, which in practice results in risk avoidance. Ignorance of risk, on the other hand, most often associated with it indifference to opportunities and threats, is associated with unawareness of the existence of risk and/or ignorance about it.

In enterprise risk management the most desirable attitude towards risk is risk taking (active attitude), which in practice consists of understanding the essence of risk, accepting its existence and acting in order to mitigate threats, and using opportunities connected with taking specific decisions. This is fostered by a positive perception of risk, confidence, and a more energetic and dynamic attitude toward the world (Brooks & Williams, 2021).

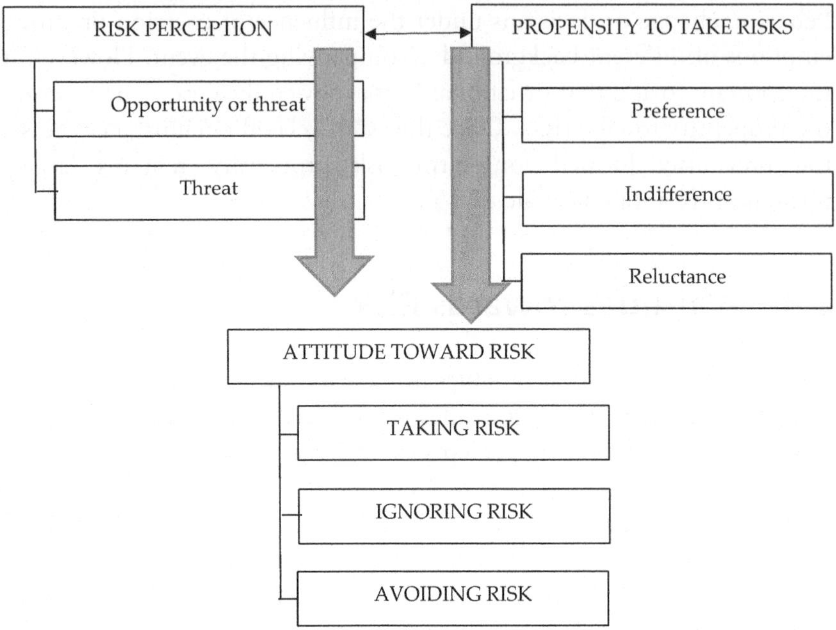

Fig. 2.1 Relationships between risk perception and propensity and attitudes toward risk. (Source: Own work based on the literature referenced in this chapter)

Risk avoidance can inhibit entrepreneurial initiatives and actions, which is a barrier to business growth. It does not always mean a lack of knowledge about risk and risk management, but only a paralyzing fear of making decisions and the associated consequences, which is caused by the determinants related to risk perception and propensity described in the previous chapters (e.g., personality traits, gender, age, experience history, nationality, etc.).

The indifferent attitude towards risk associated with ignoring threats and passive attitude towards opportunities seems to be the least desirable in risk management, due to the lack of knowledge about risk that it causes, ignorance and, consequently, not taking any action to prevent the occurrence of a threat regardless of its intensity and scale.

It is also worth mentioning that in the current market conditions of rapid flow and access to information, attitudes towards risk can be spread quickly and be a source of contagion for many participants in economic life. For these reasons—as emphasized by Qian et al. (2021), awareness and knowledge of the behavioral aspects affecting the effectiveness of risk management is extremely important.

From the considerations presented in this chapter, it is clear that risk management, and thus its effectiveness, is strongly influenced by behavioral factors directly related to the person of the decision maker. This is undoubtedly due to the behavioral theory of decision-making, although as risk is associated with threats the amplitude and scope of the decision maker's behavior may be more significant and pronounced in this case than in other management decisions.

Summarizing the previous research and considerations, it is important to state that a positive perception of risk encourages economic challenges and therefore fosters entrepreneurship, innovation and business growth (Gieure et al., 2020; Gurd & Helliar, 2017; Caggese, 2012). However, it needs to be underpinned by risk management knowledge and experience, so that excessive optimism or even bravado does not expose the enterprise to unpredictable risks and thus damage and loss. Therefore, it is also important to have an active attitude to risk, manifested not only in the preference of risky situations, but above all in the skillful prevention of threats, thereby maximizing the effectiveness of risk management in the enterprise.

References

Abou-El-Sood, H. (2021). Board gender diversity, power, and bank risk taking. *International Review of Financial Analysis, 75*, 101733.

Ameljańczyk, A. (2017). Model ewaluacji ryzyka i jego percepcji podstawą zarządzania ryzykiem. *Nowoczesne Systemy Zarządzania, 2*(2), 31–46.

Arena, M., Arnaboldi, M., & Azzone, G. (2010). The organizational dynamics of enterprise risk management. *Accounting, Organizations and Society, 35*(7), 659–675.

Astakhova, M. N., Beal, B. D., & Camp, K. M. (2017). A cross-cultural examination of the curvilinear relationship between perceived demands-abilities fit and risk-taking propensity. *Journal of Business Research, 79*, 41–51.

Bajcar, B. (2012). Kwestionariusz Styl Myślenia i Działania Strategicznego. Nowe narzędzie do pomiaru wskaźników myślenia strategicznego. *Studia Psychologiczne, 50*(2), 5–24.

Bajcar, B. (2017). Różnice indywidualne w stylach myślenia i działania strategicznego. *Studia Psychologiczne, 55*(1), 1–15.

Brooks, C., & Williams, L. (2021). The impact of personality traits on attitude to financial risk. *Research in International Business and Finance, 58*, 101501.

Brown, G. D., Largey, A., & McMullan, C. (2021). The impact of gender on risk perception: Implications for EU member states' national risk assessment processes. *International Journal of Disaster Risk Reduction, 63*, 102452.

Caggese, A. (2012). Entrepreneurial risk, investment, and innovation. *Journal of Financial Economics, 106*(2), 287–307.

Campara, J., Da Costa, N., Jr., Matsushita, R., & Da Silva, S. (2021). Two selves and two minds in a longitudinal survey of risk attitudes. *Journal of Behavioral and Experimental Finance, 29*, 100444.

Cantarella, S., Hillenbrand, C., & Ginsante, S. (2015). The role of immediate emotions in investment decisions. *NeuroPsychoEconomics Conference Proceedings*, 33.

Cho, E., Okafor, C., Ujah, N., & Zhang, L. (2021). Executives' gender-diversity, education, and firm's bankruptcy risk: Evidence from China. *Journal of Behavioral and Experimental Finance, 30*, 100500.

Cui, Y., Sun, C., Xiao, H., & Zhao, C. (2016). How to become an excellent entrepreneur: The moderating effect of risk propensity on alertness to business ideas and entrepreneurial capabilities. *Technological Forecasting and Social Change, 112*, 171–177.

Czauderna, K. (2016). Paradoksy skłonności do ryzyka. O pewnej nieścisłości teorii perspektywy. *Wiadomości Statystyczne. The Polish Statistician, 2*, 25–46.

Douglas, E. J. (2009). Perceptions—Looking at the world through entrepreneurial lenses. In A. L. Carsrud & M. Brannback (Eds.), *Understanding the entrepreneurial mind: Opening the black box* (pp. 5–25). Springer.

Gieure, C., del Mar Benavides-Espinosa, M., & Roig-Dobón, S. (2020). The entrepreneurial process: The link between intentions and behavior. *Journal of Business Research, 112*, 541–548.

Gurd, B., & Helliar, C. (2017). Looking for leaders: 'Balancing' innovation, risk and management control systems. *The British Accounting Review, 49*(1), 91–102.

Hysa, B., & Rakowska, A. (2014). Umiejętności decyzyjne jako kluczowe kompetencje w pracy kierownika administracji samorządowej. *Zeszyty Naukowe Politechniki Śląskiej, seria: Organizacja i Zarządzanie, 68*, 13–28.

Isen, A. M., & Baron, R. A. (1991). Positive effect as a factor in organizational behaviour. *Research in Organizational Behavior, 13*, 1–53.

Isen, A. M., & Geva, N. (1988). Influence of positive effect on the subjective utility of gains and losses: It is just not worth the risk. *Journal of Personality and Social Psychology, 55*, 710–717.

Jajuga, K., & Jajuga, T. (2006). *Inwestycje. Instrumenty finansowe, ryzyko finansowe. Inżynieria finansowa* (pp. 98–99). Wydawnictwo Naukowe PWN.

Jaramillo, M., & Vargas, K. L. (2019). Interpersonal comparisons and risk attitudes: An artefactual field experiment. *Economics Letters, 179*, 16–18.

Jędralska, K. (1992). *Zachowania przedsiębiorstw w sytuacjach niepewnych i ryzykownych* (Vol. 1992, pp. 73–77). Wydawnictwo Akademii Ekonomicznej w Katowicach.

Jeziorska, M. (2013). Postrzeganie ryzyka a działania ochronno-prewencyjne podmiotów narażonych na ryzyko. *Acta Universitatis Lodziensis, Folia Oeconomica, 296*, 33–39.

Jonek-Kowalska, I., & Wawiernia, A. (2016). How do Polish managers perceive and manage risk? Experience from the Silesian region. *Proceedings of the 12th European Conference on Management, Leadership and Governance ECMLG 2016*, Bucharest, Romania. Academic Publishing.

Macko, A., & Tyszka, T. (2005). Przedsiębiorczość i ryzykowanie. *Decyzje, 4*, 29–50.

Majewska-Bielecka, B. (2012). Wielokulturowy aspekt skłonności do ryzyka. *Zeszyty Naukowe Zachodniopomorskiej Szkoły Biznesu Firma i Rynek, 1*, 93–102.

Mohsni, S., Otchere, I., & Shahriar, S. (2021). Board gender diversity, firm performance and risk-taking in developing countries: The moderating effect of culture. *Journal of International Financial Markets, Institutions and Money, 73*, 101360.

Nax, H. H., & Newton, J. (2019). Risk attitudes and risk dominance in the long run. *Games and Economic Behavior, 116*, 179–184.

Ober, J. (2020). Innovation adoption: Empirical analysis on the example of selected factors of organizational culture in the IT industry in Poland. *Sustainability, 12*, 8630.

Pera, J. (2013). Zarządzanie ryzykiem i jego dywersyfikacja w świetle teorii finansów behawioralnych a model Neumanna-Morgensterna. *Zeszyty Naukowe Uniwersytetu Ekonomicznego w Krakowie, 920*, 67–81.

Pilch, I., & Rosmus, R. (2004). Osobowościowe uwarunkowania zachowań manipulacyjnych. *Chowanna, 2*, 164–175.

Qayyum, A., Rehman, I. U., Shahzad, F., Khan, N., Nawaz, F., Kokkalis, P., & Sergi, B. S. (2021). Board gender diversity and stock price crash risk: Going beyond tokenism. *Borsa Istanbul Review, 21*(3), 269–280.

Qian, Q., Feng, H., & Gu, J. (2021). The influence of risk attitude on credit risk contagion—Perspective of information dissemination. *Physica A: Statistical Mechanics and its Applications, 582*, 126226.

Sekścińska, K., Rudzinska-Wojciechowska, J., & Jaworska, S. (2021). Self-control and financial risk taking. *Journal of Economic Psychology, 85*, 102386.

Shahriar, A. Z. M. (2018). Gender differences in entrepreneurial propensity: Evidence from matrilineal and patriarchal societies. *Journal of Business Venturing, 33*(6), 762–779.

Sołtysiak, M. (2014). Menedżerowie w procesie zarządzania ryzykiem. *Modern Management Review, XIX*(2), 141–148.

Tavor, T. (2019). The theoretical attitude and actual behavior of an individual towards risk. *Journal of Behavioral and Experimental Finance, 23*, 1–11.

Tyszka, T., & Domurat, A. (2004). Czy istnieje ogólna skłonność jednostki do ryzyka? *Decyzje, 2*, 85–10.

Wang, C. M., Xu, B. B., Zhang, S. J., & Chen, Y. Q. (2016). Influence of personality and risk propensity on risk perception of Chinese construction project managers. *International Journal of Project Management, 34*(7), 1294–1304.

Wieczorek, I. (2013). Ekonomiczne aspekty ryzyka. In: Współczesna ekonomia wobec załamania koniunktury gospodarczej, K. Koj, J. Szostak (Eds.). *Zeszyty Naukowe Wydziału Zamiejscowego w Chorzowie Wyższej Szkoły Bankowej w Poznaniu, 15*, 163–182.

Wiśniewska-Szatek, A. (2005). Percepcja i podejmowanie ryzyka przez menedżerów. *Organizacje Komercyjne i Niekomercyjne wobec Wzmożonej Konkurencji i Rosnących Wymagań Konsumenta, 4*, 293–302.

Wyrozębski, P., Juchniewicz, M., & Metelski, W. (2012). *Wiedza, dojrzałość, ryzyko w zarządzaniu projektami—wyniki badań*. Oficyna Wydawnicza SGH.

Zhang, Q., & Li, Z. (2021). Time-varying risk attitude and the foreign exchange market behavior. *Research in International Business and Finance, 57*, 101394.

Zhu, D., Hodgkinson, L., & Wang, Q. (2021). Interaction and decomposition of gender difference in financial risk perception. *Journal of Behavioral and Experimental Finance, 30*, 100464.

3

Endogenous Determinants of Risk Management Effectiveness

3.1 Risk Management Process and Methodology

As highlighted in Chap. 1, risk management is a complex and multi-step process. Its scope is decided by enterprise managers in the context of two key issues, i.e.:

1. The selection and choice of risk management methods and the systematization of the enterprise risk management process;
2. Type and scale of human and financial resources involved in the defined risk management process.

Both issues are qualified as internal determinants of the effectiveness of enterprise risk management and characterized in this chapter.

As it is known, risk management is a structured process, which means that it follows sequential steps and is equipped with a set of specific methods and tools. However, these methods and tools differ depending on the stage of risk management. Thus, the sample tools shown in Fig. 3.1 can be used in **threats identification** to identify sources of risk.

I. Jonek-Kowalska, *Effectiveness of Enterprise Risk Management*,
https://doi.org/10.1007/978-3-030-95376-8_3

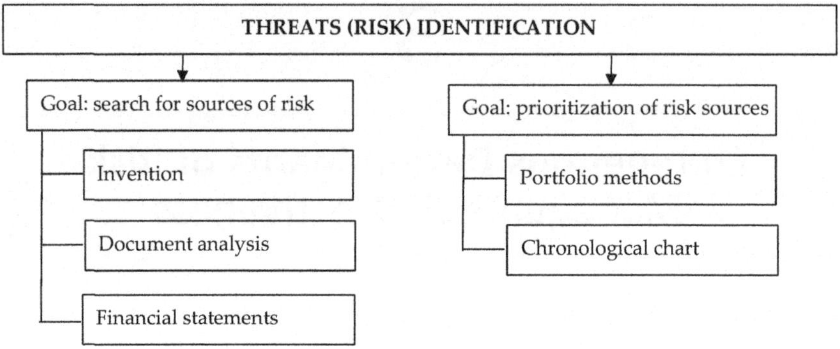

Fig. 3.1 Examples of threats identification methods in a company. (Source: Own work based on the literature referenced in this chapter)

When searching for sources of risk inside and around the company, it is very helpful to use inventive methods, including, above all, brainstorming and the involvement of as many experts as possible who identify sources of risk in different areas of the company's activities. This allows determining the broadest possible catalog of potential threats, which is crucial for further stages of risk management, and consequently for the effectiveness of the process. This is because inventive methods allow (Proctor, 2002; Nęcka, 1994; Antoszkiewicz, 1990; Martyniak, 1990; Osborn 1963):

- Discovering new sources of risk.
- Finding creative solutions to problems.
- Identifying multifaceted connections between facts and events.
- Formulating hypotheses.
- Predicting the course of events and estimating the consequences of such events.

The above mentioned features of these methods make them very useful in identifying risks, which by their nature are difficult to predict and require a broad and multidimensional research perspective.

While searching for sources of risk, it is also helpful to analyze events in historical terms conducted on the basis of company documentation, including financial statements (Skrzypek, 2010; Grajewski, 2007). It allows not only to estimate the frequency of occurrence of specific threats, but also a preliminary assessment of damages and losses associated with their occurrence, which can be used in risk assessment.

The above methods allow creating and completing the risk checklist, but do not allow to systematize it. They are also static in nature. Therefore, in order to dynamize and organize the sources of risk, it is useful to use the chronological chart method, which refers to process-based business management (Williams et al., 2002). In this method, all processes are mapped (van den Brink et al., 2020; Trucco et al., 2015), their stages are distinguished, and then sources of potential risks and losses are assigned to them.

Systematization and prioritization of sources of risk in an enterprise are also enabled by portfolio methods (Hassel & Cedergren, 2021; Teller & Kock, 2021). A measurable result of these methods are risk matrices. In these matrices, individual sources of risk are assigned descriptive scores that allow prioritizing the sources of risk and determining their impact on the business. This is an important element of risk valuation and its preliminary assessment.

Regardless of the type of adopted threats (risk) identification methodology, managers should remember that the search for sources of threats and losses cannot be a one-time activity, due to the volatility, abundance and unpredictability of risk sources, as evidenced by the example of the global crisis caused by the coronavirus pandemic and the increasing number of natural disasters caused by the climate crisis. Threats identification, therefore, must be a cyclically repeated and carefully prepared step to ensure that the company continues to monitor potential risks.

The threats identification output, which is a checklist of hazards (Albris et al., 2020; Rosecrance et al., 2017), is the starting point for estimating the probability and extent of damage and loss caused by the occurrence of the identified hazards. This estimation is the basis for the **risk assessment** using the following methods:

- Qualitative,
- Quantitative,
- Mixed.

Quantitative methods include probabilistic, statistical and econometric methods (Sienkiewicz, 2010). The former are based on probability calculus. Using them, the probability of occurrence of particular sources of risk in the future is estimated (Wang et al., 2021; Li et al., 2019). A company, having information about risks and losses, is additionally able to determine the scale of the consequences of risk realization. However, the use of probability calculus requires knowledge of the past or expected frequency of events and information about the effects of these events. In the first case, the information used is burdened by the not always true assumption of repeatability of the past, while in the second case it is burdened by the impossibility of precise prediction of the future. Risk estimation will therefore always be accompanied by forecast error (Jonek-Kowalska, 2017).

In statistical methods, risk estimation takes place primarily in the context of the variability of a phenomenon (Witkowski, 2009). The higher the variability over time, the higher the risk. Common measures of variability are used for measurement. These methods, as well as probabilistic ones, are accompanied by forecast error resulting from basing measurements on historical or predicted data.

Econometric methods use specific econometric functions to estimate risk. Among the most commonly used are functions allowing for sensitivity analysis, discriminant analysis, as well as multiple regression functions (Saltelli et al., 2000, 2008; Saisana et al., 2005). Sensitivity analysis determines the strength of the response of an output variable to changes in the magnitude of an input variable. This response identifies the intensity of risk in the business. The more rapid the response, the higher the risk. Discriminant analysis, on the other hand, classifies companies according to the level of risk associated with their activities. The functions used in its performance usually include the most relevant indicators of the assessment of the financial condition of the company. Discriminant analysis is used primarily in assessing the risk of bankruptcy (Hołda, 2001). On the basis of its results, analyzed entities are divided into those threatened with bankruptcy and those not threatened with bankruptcy. An extension of discriminant analysis are multiple regression functions, which allow to estimate bankruptcy risk in a more precise way by indicating the degree of bankruptcy risk (Jonek-Kowalska, 2017).

In qualitative methods, risk is not quantified. The risk assessment takes the form of a description. The identified risk factors are assigned intuitively estimated levels, for example "low risk, average risk, high risk". Descriptive risk assessment methods can also be called expert methods, as they are based on the opinions of specialists and/or the company's management. Their main disadvantage is the subjectivity of the assessment, while the advantage is the simplicity and speed of application. They are considered less precise than quantitative methods. However, it should be remembered that quantitative methods based on false assumptions and/or using incorrect data may provide incorrect assessments of the level of risk, and thus prove less accurate than qualitative methods. Therefore, one should not place undue confidence in the results of quantitative methods if there is uncertainty about the quality of the assumptions and data used in them. Dogmatic preference for quantitative methods can become the cause of many management errors, leading in extreme cases to the collapse of the company (Nocera, 2009; Kolman et al., 1998). Therefore, as a preventive measure, quantitative results of risk estimation should be confronted with the results obtained using qualitative methods, taking into account the experience of experts, and then determine the reasons for the discrepancies.

Taking into account the disadvantages of individual quantitative and qualitative methods, the company can use mixed variants, combining selected methods of quantitative and qualitative risk assessment. Examples of quantitative and qualitative risk assessment tools with their brief characteristics are presented in Table 3.1.

Currently, there is an increase in mathematization (Lin et al., 2021) of individual methods and individualized approach to the assessment of individual sources of risk. This makes it possible to increase the precision of the estimates made, but at the same time limits the applicability of the proposed solutions. These methods require a lot of input data—not always in the possession of the company—increasing the time and cost of calculations. Moreover, their internal construction is very often understandable only for a very narrow group of experts, so in practice it requires specialized IT infrastructure. This limits the group of companies that can implement the proposed methods. Excessive mathematization of risk assessment is also associated with the mentioned excessive confidence in

Table 3.1 Classification of qualitative and quantitative risk assessment tools in a company

Qualitative methods	Quantitative methods
Scenario methods which involve drawing up three variants of scenarios showing the probable course of events and risks in pessimistic, optimistic and realistic terms.	Probabilistic measures using probability calculus to estimate the frequency of events.
Rating methods that make it possible to divide companies into various risk classes—from the lowest to the highest, depending on the rules of evaluation and the evaluating entity (ratings usually refer to the risk of corporate insolvency).	Volatility measures using descriptive statistics according to the principle of the higher the volatility, the higher the risk.
Risk mapping based on risk checklists made as part of threats identyfication to develop a risk map that synthetically and clearly illustrates individual sources of risk and their level in the company.	Discriminant analysis used in solving classification problems of sets of varying characteristics.
Risk matrix, which is a form of risk map that takes into account the probability of risk occurrence and the consequences of its occurrence and allows to create risk categories.	Capital Asset Pricing Model (CAPM): using β coefficient, which determines the level of market risk associated with investing in the assets of a specific company.
SWOT/PESTEL analysis SWOT as a list of weaknesses, strengths, threats and opportunities expanded with parametric assessment can provide a starting point for ranking individual sources of risk. PESTEL makes it possible to classify the sources of risk identified in individual segments and then assess them using either qualitative or quantitative methods.	The Value At Risk (VaR) method is used in short-term analyses on the financial market, based on the evaluation of the volatility of the company's assets (the higher the value, the higher the risk for the company).

(*continued*)

Table 3.1 (continued)

Qualitative methods	Quantitative methods
SPACE (Strategic Position and Action Evaluation) method is a development of SWOT analysis used to identify those sources of risk that hinder company's development.	Monte-Carlo method which is an improved version of VaR and makes it possible to analyze a very large number of changes in the value of assets, taking into account their correlation.
Scoring methods based on indicators integral to risk assessment (e.g., liquidity, profitability, etc.), which are assigned a score (the sum of points awarded for all indicators taken into account in the assessment indicates a predefined risk class).	Capital At Risk (CaR) is an extension of VaR that makes it possible to determine the value of capital necessary to secure an enterprise in the event of maximum loss.
HAZOP method (Hazards and Operability Study) used to assess the technical risk in investment projects of an enterprise and oriented towards the protection of material and human resources against the risks associated with the physical implementation of the investment.	Risk-Adjusted Return On Capital (RAROC) is a development of CaR and allows to determine the risk-adjusted rate of return on capital (then the expected return on the investment is reduced by the hedging capital and increased by the return on the investment of this capital, so adjusted return is related to the capital at risk).
	Risk MetricsTM advanced mathematical and IT risk assessment instrumentation based on VaR assumptions.

Source: Own elaboration on the literature referenced in this chapter

the final results, which without prior rational and critical verification become the only basis for management decisions.

Once the risk is identified and assessed, the company must decide on the **actions it intends to take in the area of risk**. These actions include physical and/or financial risk control. Within tangible risk control, a distinction is made between

- risk avoidance and
- risk prevention.

Risk avoidance occurs when a company refuses to accept even temporary risks. Then no risk is accepted and the previously accepted risk is rejected (Michalski, 2000). This is not a recommended attitude, nevertheless, it can often be found in practice, especially in small and medium-sized enterprises that use risk management methods and tools to a limited extent. It is also worth noting that risk avoidance significantly reduces the cost of risk management as the company does not take any action, thus incurring no expenses. Risk avoidance has a negative impact on the effectiveness of risk management as it implies a passive attitude to risks and a lack of preventive action to mitigate risks.

The opposite of risk avoidance in the area of physical control is prevention of the risk referred to as risk prevention (Kowalewski, 1994). In this case, the company takes proactive measures to prevent damage and/or reduce its frequency and final size (Di Ludovico & Di Lodovico, 2020). Managers then focus on actions that prevent the realization of a given risk or hinder the occurrence of a concrete hazard. A typical example of preventive action is the application of fire safety regulations and measures or occupational health and safety regulations.

In addition to material risk control, a company may use financial control, which includes

- risk retention and
- risk transfer.

Financial risk control supports tangible methods of risk mitigation by minimizing the consequences of risk occurrence (Bodie and Merton, 2003; Łuczak, 2003). It also creates opportunities to reduce risks taken intentionally, the so-called speculative risks. In case of risk transfer, the consequences of risk occurrence or its financial consequences are transferred to another entity. It can be, and most often is, an insurance company, but this role can also be played by a supplier, customer or cooperator of the company. Risk transfer can also take the form of hedging or diversification, that is, spreading the effects of a risk over a larger number of entities.

Risk transfer contributes to more effective risk management by reducing damage and loss to business. However, like prevention, it involves additional costs and procedures. Classic examples of the cost of risk transfer are insurance premiums, fees related to cooperation agreements or derivative transactions.

Risk retention may be associated with a conscious decision, or it may be the result of lack of knowledge about the risk and the consequences of its occurrence (Łukasik, 2004). In the first case, we deal with active risk retention. Then the managers consciously decide not to prevent or use the transfer and take over the risk partially or completely. Such a decision is often based on financial motives, such as lack of funds to pay premiums or purchase physical security. There may also be non-financial motives in the form of lack of transfer or prevention tools. Whatever the reason, a company should make sure that it has the means to cover all or at least part of the potential losses that may occur if the risk is realized, so as to prevent disruption to operations or, in extreme cases, bankruptcy.

In practice, passive risk retention resulting from indifference to risks and ignoring risks is also possible. It is very dangerous for the continuity of the company's operation, may cause serious financial losses and even lead to bankruptcy. It is also worth mentioning that neither active nor passive risk retention is conducive to effective risk management, as it involves more or less conscious abandonment of actions aimed at mitigating risks.

It is also worth mentioning that in medium and large enterprises risk management methods and tools take the form of advanced procedures often supported by computer software. They create what is known as *Enterprise Risk Management* (ERM) systems. These systems collect multidimensional risk data, which very often are processed through complex computational techniques using IT tools (Jonek-Kowalska, 2019; Dudlák, 2018; Frangou et al., 2018; Conrad & Kostka, 2017; Collier, 2009). Based on the obtained data, a risk management methodology is designed covering all resources and processes of the enterprise. The detail with the holistic nature of ERM systems is intended to increase the effectiveness of enterprise risk management. However, the implementation of such systems is capital-intensive and requires expert knowledge, which is why they are more common in large business entities.

The final stage of risk management is **control**, which in practice boils down to evaluation of effectiveness and efficiency. Control should be conducted in a systematic manner to lead to the company's constant improvement of its identification, assessment and action on risks. Examples of tools used in the course of risk management control are (Chandra & Calderon, 2009):

- Risk reaction audits.
- Periodic risk reviews.
- Summary of technical measurements.
- Description s of risk reactions.
- Statements of damages and losses.

The relevant references emphasize that proper planning, preparation and implementation of the risk management process contributes to the success of the company's intentions and improved business results (Vujović et al., 2020). Nevertheless, an instrumental approach to risk management is not a sufficient guarantee of effective protection against risks. Indeed, many studies show that without the involvement of human resources in risk management, the plans and successes of the enterprise are seriously compromised (Agarwal & Rathod, 2006; Atkinson, 1999; Turner, 1993). The role and importance of managers and employees in the described context is detailed in the next section.

3.2 Resources Involved in Risk Management

For risk management to be effective and efficient, i.e. to contribute to reducing the sources of risk and/or offsetting the effects of risk realization with optimal resource commitment, knowledge and experience on risk management methods and systems are essential, which allow the planning of risk reduction activities and their proper implementation.

The scope of risk management methods implemented in an enterprise depends on, among other things: the size of the enterprise, the type of business it conducts, and the human and financial resources at its disposal (Haas & Yorio, 2019; Arnold et al., 2015).

Human resources in the risk management process have a very important function, as they are carriers of risk knowledge linked to the behavioral determinants described earlier and resulting from previous experience and education in risk management. A study by Okudan et al. (2021) shows that extensive knowledge and familiarity with good risk management practices contributes to the improvement and effectiveness of enterprise risk management, and the involvement of human resources in threats identyfication and assessment can result in a reduction in the enterprise's risk exposure (Dikmen et al., 2008). For these reasons, the accumulation of risk knowledge both in the minds of employees and the collective memory of the organization is one of the key factors affecting the effectiveness of enterprise risk management (Lu et al., 2013; Kivrak et al., 2008).

Research and deliberations also emphasize the importance of proper communication in risk management, which is an important reinforcement of the methodical and instrumental aspect of risk management. Achieving effective protection against risks is therefore only possible when appropriate risk management techniques are accompanied by effective interpersonal communication (Bakker et al., 2012).

The involvement of human resources in risk management can vary in scope, so this monograph assumes that the lowest level of risk management refers to the situation in which a company does not employ risk management specialists, entrusting some of the responsibilities related to this process (e.g., occupational health and safety) to employees or units that also perform other activities (e.g., human resources). A higher degree of risk protection is achieved by employing professional risk management experts and by having a dedicated risk management function within the enterprise.

The highest level of advancement in this area is the development and implementation of the already mentioned holistic risk management systems, or in other words, *Enterprise Risk Management (ERM)*, covering monitoring and protection of the entire enterprise. These systems can be created within the company with the involvement of its employees' knowledge and experience, or they can be created by consulting companies that design and implement them on a daily basis (Sienou et al., 2020). It should also be added that in advanced risk management systems all employees of the company are aware of the existence of such a system, participate in its creation and improvement, continuously identify and monitor risks, report on potential threats and contribute to increasing the level of protection.

Despite the relatively small number of publications devoted to the effectiveness and efficiency of individual risk management methods and systems, it is assumed that as the sophistication of risk management increases, so does the level of protection against adverse consequences associated with the realization of risk. This is also confirmed by previous research (de Araújo Lima et al., 2020). Thus, risk management methods and systems are an important element in the management of a modern enterprise to adapt more efficiently and effectively to changes in the environment (Malik et al., 2020; Singh & Hong, 2020).

The results of previous studies indicate that small and medium-sized enterprises mainly use their own knowledge and intuition in risk mitigation, do not use advanced methods, nor do they use integrated risk management systems or project-based risk management methodologies. This is mainly due to the time- and cost-consuming nature of designing and implementing these systems, as well as the belief that they can handle all risks on their own. Importantly, however, international studies also show that this approach is insufficient and relying only on the internal knowledge of managers of small and medium-sized enterprises does not enable effective risk management, even when organizational structures and risk exposures appear to be small (Hock-Doepgen et al., 2020; Cantonnet et al., 2019).

As already mentioned, holistic risk management systems or ERM, are generally used in large companies. Their implementation and operation involves a series of internal procedures related to threats identyfication, assessment, reporting and monitoring (Nguyen & Vo, 2019). In theory, such an approach is comprehensive and so should be the enterprise protection guaranteed by its existence. Nevertheless, in practice, risk management with ERM often becomes just another documentation routine and an additional element to improve the media image.

Meanwhile, in risk management, both ignorance of risk and a routine approach to its identification and assessment can contribute to very serious consequences, including bankruptcy.

Indeed, in today's globalized economies, events occur that are difficult to predict, such as the collapse triggered by the 2008 US mortgage crisis or the 2019 coronavirus pandemic. Awareness of the unpredictability of risk and its consequences cannot be a rationale for not planning for an emergency, as the consequences in this regard can be very serious for both companies and entire economies. For these reasons, both the risk management methodology and the commitment of human resources to its implementation are important determinants of the effectiveness and efficiency of risk management. These determinants will be included in the research model described in the empirical part of the paper.

References

Agarwal, N., & Rathod, U. (2006). Defining 'success' for software projects: An exploratory revelation. *International Journal of Project Management, 24*(4), 358–370.

Albris, K., Cedervall, K., & Raju, L. A. (2020). Strengthening governance for disaster prevention: The enhancing risk management capabilities guidelines. *International Journal of Disaster Risk Reduction, 47*, 101647.

Antoszkiewicz, J. (1990). *Metody heurystyczne. Twórcze rozwiązywanie problemów*. Wydawnictwo PWE.

Arnold, V., Benford, T., Canada, J., & Sutton, S. G. (2015). Leveraging integrated information systems to enhance strategic flexibility and performance: The enabling role of enterprise risk management. *International Journal of Accounting Information Systems, 19*, 1–16.

Atkinson, R. (1999). Project management: Cost, time and quality, two best guesses and a phenomenon, it's time to accept other success criteria. *International Journal of Project Management, 17*(6), 337–342.

Bakker, K., Boonstra, A., & Wortmann, H. (2012). Risk managements' communicative effects influencing IT project success. *International Journal of Project Management, 30*(4), 444–457.

Bodie, Z., & Merton, R. G. (2003). *Finanse*. PWE.

Cantonnet, M. L., Aldasoro, J. C., & Iradi, J. (2019). New and emerging risks management in small and medium-sized Spanish enterprises. *Safety Science, 113*, 257–263.

Chandra, A., & Calderon, T. G. (2009). Information intensity, control deficiency risk, and materiality. *Managerial Auditing Journal, 24*(3), 220–232.
Collier, P. M. (2009). Towards Enterprise risk management. In *Fundamentals of risk management for accountants and managers. Tools & techniques* (pp. 45–57). Elsevier Ltd.
Conrad, B., & Kostka, G. (2017). Chinese investments in Europe's energy sector: Risks and opportunities? *Energy Policy, 101*, 644–648.
De Araújo Lima, P. F., Crema, M., & Verbano, C. (2020). Risk management in SMEs: A systematic literature review and future directions. *European Management Journal, 38*, 78–94.
Di Ludovico, D., & Di Lodovico, L. (2020). The Regional Management Risk Plan. Knowledge, scenarios and prevention projects in a regional context. *International Journal of Disaster Risk Reduction, 45*, 101465.
Dikmen, I., Birgonul, M. T., Anac, C., Tah, J. H. M., & Aouad, G. (2008). Learning from risks: A tool for post-project risk assessment. *Automation in Construction, 18*(1), 42–50.
Dudlák, T. (2018). After the sanctions: Policy challenges in transition to a new political economy of the Iranian oil and gas sectors. *Energy Policy, 121*, 464–475.
Frangou, M., Aryblia, M., Tournaki, S., & Tsoutsos, T. (2018). Renewable energy performance contracting in the tertiary sector. Standardization to overcome barriers in Greece. *Renewable Energy, 125*, 829–839.
Grajewski, P. (2007). *Organizacja procesowa*. PWE.
Haas, E. M., & Yorio, P. L. (2019). The role of risk avoidance and locus of control in workers' near miss experiences: Implications for improving safety management systems. *Journal of Loss Prevention in the Process Industries, 59*, 91–99.
Hassel, H., & Cedergren, A. (2021). Integrating risk assessment and business impact assessment in the public crisis management sector. *International Journal of Disaster Risk Reduction, 56*(1), 102136.
Hock-Doepgen, M., Clauss, T., Kraus, S., & Cheng, C.-F. (2020). Knowledge management capabilities and organizational risk-taking for business model innovation in SMEs. *Journal of Business Research, 130*, 683–697.
Hołda, A. (2001). Wykorzystanie analizy dyskryminacyjnej w predykcji bankructwa—doświadczenia światowe. *Zeszyty Teoretyczne Rachunkowości, 5*(61), 59–69.
Jonek-Kowalska, I. (2017). *Prowartościowe kształtowanie parametrów produkcji górniczej w warunkach ryzyka branżowego i rynkowego*. Wydawnictwo Politechniki Śląskiej w Gliwicach.

Jonek-Kowalska, I. (2019). Efficiency of Enterprise Risk Management (ERM) systems. Comparative analysis in the fuel sector and energy sector on the basis of Central-European companies listed on the Warsaw Stock Exchange. *Resources Policy, 62*, 405–415.

Kivrak, S., Arslan, G., Dikmen, I., & Birgonul, M. T. (2008). Capturing knowledge in construction projects: Knowledge platform for contractors. *Journal of Management in Engineering, 24*(2), 87–95.

Kolman, J., Onak, M., Jorion, P., Taleb, N., & Derman, E. (1998, April). Roundtable: The limits of VaR. *Derivatives Strategy*.

Kowalewski, E. (1994). *Wprowadzenie do teorii ryzyka ubezpieczeniowego*. [W:] A. Wąsiewicz (Ed.), *Ubezpieczenia w gospodarce rynkowej*. Wydawnictwo Branta.

Li, H., Huang, Y., & Tian, S. (2019). Risk probability predictions for coal enterprise infrastructure projects in countries along the Belt and Road Initiative. *International Journal of Industrial Ergonomics, 69*, 110–117.

Lin, S.-S., Shen, S.-L., Zhou, A., & Xu, Y.-S. (2021). Risk assessment and management of excavation system based on fuzzy set theory and machine learning methods. *Automation in Construction, 122*, 103490.

Lu, Y., Li, Q., & Xiao, W. (2013). Case-based reasoning for automated safety risk analysis on subway operation: Case representation and retrieval. *Safety Science, 57*, 75–81.

Łuczak, M. (2003). *Ryzyko i kryzys w zarządzaniu przedsiębiorstwem*. Wyższa Szkoła Ekonomiczna.

Łukasik, G. (2004). *Strategie przedsiębiorstwa w sytuacjach kryzysowych*. Wydawnictwo Akademii Ekonomicznej w Katowicach.

Malik, M. F., Zaman, M., & Buckby, S. (2020). Enterprise risk management and firm performance: Role of the risk committee. *Journal of Contemporary Accounting & Economics, 16*, 100178.

Martyniak, Z. (1990). *Inwentyka przemysłowa*. Wydawnictwo IWZZ.

Michalski, T. (2000). *Ryzyko w działalności człowieka*. [W:] J. Monkiewicz (Ed.), *Podstawy ubezpieczeń. Mechanizmy i funkcje*. Poltext.

Nęcka, E. (1994). *Twórcze rozwiązywanie problemów*. Wydawnictwo Impuls.

Nguyen, D. K., & Vo, D. T. (2019). Enterprise risk management and solvency: The case of the listed EU insurers. *Journal of Business Research, 113*, 360–369.

Nocera, J. (2009, January 4). Risk Mismanagement. *The New York Times Magazine*.

Okudan, O., Budayan, C., & Dikmen, I. (2021). A knowledge-based risk management tool for construction projects using case-based reasoning. *Expert Systems with Applications, 173*, 114776.

Osborn, A. F. (1963). *Applied imagination: Principles and procedures of creative problem solving*. Charles Scribner's Sons.

Proctor, T. (2002). *Twórcze rozwiązywanie problemów*. Wydawnictwo GWP.

Rosecrance, J., Paulsen, R., & Murgia, L. (2017). Risk assessment of cheese processing tasks using the Strain Index and OCRA Checklist. *International Journal of Industrial Ergonomics, 61*, 142–148.

Saisana, M., Saltelli, A., & Tarantola, S. (2005). Uncertainty and sensitivity analysis techniques as tools for the quality assessment of composite indicators. *Journal of the Royal Statistical Society, 168*(2), 307–323.

Saltelli, A., Chan, K., & Scott, M. (2000). *Sensitivity analysis*. Wiley Series in Probability and Statistics.

Saltelli, A., Ratto, M., Andres, T., Campolongo, F., Cariboni, J., Gatelli, D., Saisana, M., & Tarantola, S. (2008). *Global sensitivity analysis. The primer*. John Wiley & Sons.

Sienkiewicz, P. (2010). *Ewaluacja ryzyka w zarządzaniu kryzysowym*. [W:] *Ryzyko w zarządzaniu kryzysowym* (P. Sienkiewicz, M. Marszałek, & P. Górny, Eds.). Wydawnictwo A. Marszałek.

Sienou, A., Bork, D., & Pingaud, H. (2020). BPRIM: An integrated framework for business process management and risk management. *Computers in Industry, 117*, 103199.

Singh, N. P., & Hong, P. C. (2020). Impact of strategic and operational risk management practices on firm performance: An empirical investigation. *European Management Journal* (Vol. 38(5), pp. 723–735). In press. Available online 6 March 2020.

Skrzypek, E. (2010). *Zarządzanie procesami w przedsiębiorstwie*. Wolters Kluwer.

Teller, J., & Kock, A. (2021). An empirical investigation on how portfolio risk management influences project portfolio success. *International Journal of Project Management, 31*(6), 817–829.

Trucco, P., De Ambroggi, M., & Leva, M. C. (2015). Topological risk mapping of runway overruns: A probabilistic approach. *Reliability Engineering & System Safety, 142*, 433–443.

Turner, J. R. (1993). *The handbook of project based management*. McGraw-Hill.

Van den Brink, S., Kleijn, R., Sprecher, B., & Tukker, A. (2020). Identifying supply risks by mapping the cobalt supply chain. *Resources, Conservation and Recycling, 156*, 104743.

Vujović, V., Denić, N., Stevanović, V., Stevanović, M., Stojanović, J., Cao, Y., Alhammadi, Y., Jermsittiparsertef, K., Van Leg, H., Wakil, K., & Radojkovic, I. (2020). Project planning and risk management as a success factor for IT projects in agricultural schools in Serbia. *Technology in Society, 63*, 101371.

Wang, L., Ma, F., Haoa, J., & Gao, X. (2021). Forecasting crude oil volatility with geopolitical risk: Do time-varying switching probabilities play a role? *International Review of Financial Analysis, 76*, 101756.

Williams, C. A., Smith, M. L., & Young, P. C. (2002). *Zarządzanie ryzykiem a ubezpieczenia*. Wydawnictwo Naukowe PWN.

Witkowski, M. (2009). *Ryzyko gospodarcze i jego pomiar. Zagadnienia wybrane*. Wydawnictwo PWSZ w Kaliszu.

4

Exogenous Determinants of Risk Management Effectiveness

4.1 The Proximal Environment as a Source of Risk in Enterprise Operations

The enterprise is not an entity that solely operates on the basis of its own resources and internal processes. It functions in a specific economic environment which significantly affects its operational and strategic situation. The environment as a source of opportunities and threats also has a direct impact on the achievement of the enterprise's goals. In current market conditions, this impact is particularly intense due to the progressive internationalisation of economies and internationalisation of the activities of enterprises (El Namaki, 2014). The indicated circumstances contribute to the rapid diffusion and accumulation of risk (Bakkar & Nyola, 2021; Sun et al., 2020; Figueira-de-Lemos et al., 2011).

The environment of the enterprise (Ansoff et al., 2019; Ansoff, 2007; Williamson et al., 2004) consists of two elements and their internal segments schematically presented in Fig. 4.1.

Sources of risk related to the environment of the enterprise can be characterised within the segments presented in Fig. 4.1, in the context of two basic elements related to the proximal and distal environment. It is

I. Jonek-Kowalska, *Effectiveness of Enterprise Risk Management*,
https://doi.org/10.1007/978-3-030-95376-8_4

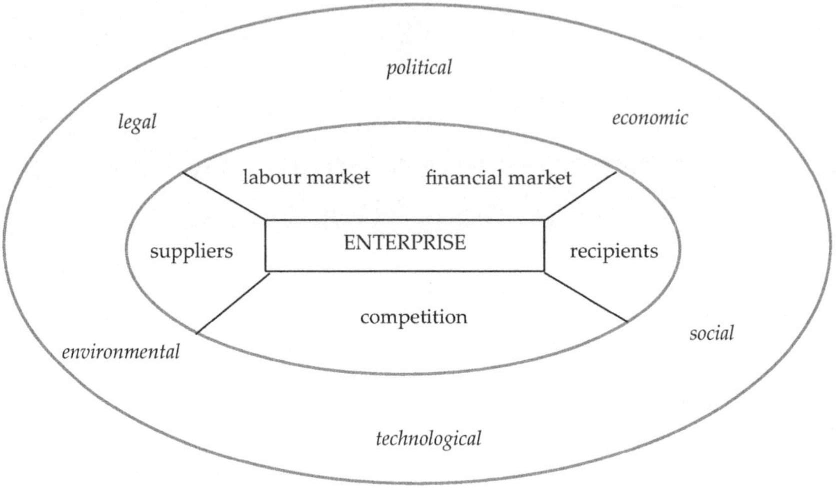

Fig. 4.1 Segments of the proximal (competitive) and distal (economic) environment of the enterprise. (Source: Own work)

from this perspective that they will be described later in this chapter and will be incorporated into the developed research model.

Its recipients and suppliers are in the proximal environment of the enterprise. The former are a source of income. The size and the selling price depend on their preferences and decisions. The latter are the source of costs for the enterprise related to the necessity to purchase raw materials, materials or services. The continuity of production and/or provision of services also depends on their willingness to cooperate. Therefore, the enterprise's contacts with suppliers and recipients shape the effectiveness of the value chain. Any disruptions and unplanned deviations in the area of these contacts are a source of risk for the achievement of the enterprise's goals, including, in particular, its financial result (Nudurupati et al., 2021; Gaganis et al., 2018; Prajogo, 2016).

An important element of the proximal environment is also the enterprise's competition, i.e. entities providing the same products and services or their substitutes (Rusten & Bryson, 2010; Sengupta, 2004; Cvitkovic, 1993). Actions taken by competitors limit the sales market and affect the level of prices in a given sector. The larger and stronger the competition, the more serious threats it generates towards the enterprise's operations.

The analysis of the proximal environment, and thus the analysis of possible threats and losses, can be carried out using Porter's five forces model (Yunna & Yisheng, 2014; Porter, 1992; Romanowska, 2015; Morrison & Roth, 1993), which includes:

1. the power of supplier influence and the possibility of them exerting pressure on enterprises in the sector;
2. the power of buyer influence and the possibility of them exerting pressure on enterprises in the sector;
3. intensification of competition within the sector;
4. the threat of the emergence of new competitors;
5. the threat of the emergence of substitutes.

Therefore, apart from entities traditionally and currently operating in the proximal environment, the risk assessment should also take into account the possibility of the emergence of new competition and substitutes for products/services that meet the expectations of buyers either to a similar extent or better.

It is worth noting that in Fig. 4.1, in the segment related to the proximal environment, the labour market and the financial market are also taken into account, which are a source of human capital and financial capital for the enterprise. Both of these capitals are necessary for the proper functioning of the enterprise both in the short and long term. Thus, the functioning of these markets significantly determines the enterprise's development opportunities.

Table 4.1 presents the potential threats related to individual segments of the proximal environment, which do not exhaust the catalogue of potential risks, but refer to its most popular components.

Apart from the risk sources listed in Table 4.1, it is worth mentioning in the context of the proximal environment the risk of loss of financial liquidity, which appears at the interface between the interior of the enterprise and the proximal environment (Población García, 2017; van der Merwe, 2015; Banks, 2014). This is the most serious risk associated with business activity. It is also the most common cause of corporate bankruptcy (du Jardin, Ph., 2021; Nishihara & Shibata, 2020). The risk of financial liquidity is associated with the possibility of losing the ability to

Table 4.1 Potential sources of risk related to individual segments of the proximal environment

Environment segment	Potential sources of risk
Suppliers	Delays in supplies. Shortage of supplies. Too high price of supplies generating unplanned costs. Inadequate quality of supplies. Disruptions in the flow of information in the supply chain. No supplier loyalty.
Recipients	Lack of matching offer to needs. Overproduction/shortage in production/service. Bad quality. Too high price. Variation of tastes/preferences. Seasonality of products/services.
Competition	Limitation of the sales market. Takeover of the sales market. Dumping. Unethical activities. High/growing requirements to enter the sector.
Labour market	Lack of desired qualifications among employees. No staff. Excessive wage/employment expectations. Unfavourable legal regulations.
Financial market	High cost of raising capital. Formal difficulties in accessing sources of financing. High requirements in the creditworthiness assessment process. Interest rate changes. Changes in currency exchange rates. Poorly developed banking system and / or financial market. Variation/lack of desired legal regulations.

Source: Own work

settle current liabilities, i.e. payments for supplies and/or work. In such cases, the enterprise loses the ability to maintain the continuity of production, and thus generate revenues and profits, and, as a consequence, is forced to stop its operations.

Loss of financial liquidity may be the result of wrong management decisions leading to the reduction of own internal sources of financing in the form of financial result. It may also result from a change in the industry situation, loss of the sales market and / or lack of access to short term sources of financing. Due to the multiplicity and diversity of causes and the intertwining of various threats, the genesis of the risk of loss of financial liquidity may be both endogenous and exogenous.

When analysing the proximal environment as a source of risk, it is worth pointing out that the enterprise has limited possibilities of influencing the functioning of this environment. Although it is an active participant, it has to adapt to the rules prevailing in the industry, co-created by other entities. It should also be added that the larger a given industry is, the smaller the possibilities are of shaping the environment by the enterprise. This is a serious obstacle in the process of threats identyfication and assessment, which is also complicated by the selection of methods and tools to mitigate individual risks. In turn, this may adversely affect the effectiveness of risk management in the enterprise.

4.2 The Distal Environment as a Source of Risk in Enterprise Operations

Contrary to the proximal environment, the distal environment is common to all enterprises and covers the general, socio-economic conditions of running a business in a given country (Geisler, 2022; Beynon-Davies, 2021; Rong & Shi, 2015). Most often, segmentation of this environment is carried out in accordance with the PESTEL analysis, which allows to distinguish the environment:

- **P**olitical,
- **E**conomic,
- **S**ocial,
- **T**echnological,
- **E**nvironmental,
- **L**egal.

The political environment primarily relates to the mechanism of state interference in the economy, i.e. the proportion between laissez-faire and government intervention. It also concerns the adopted economic system regulating the sphere of production and redistribution of goods and services in a given economy. Conditions related to the political environment also include the principles of operation of the public sector and the possibilities and scope of providing citizens with public goods (national defence, public administration, sanitary protection) and social goods (education, health care, culture) (Stabryła, 2000).

Conditions generated by the economic environment relate to the following issues:

- the business cycle and the level of gross domestic product (GDP),
- unemployment and inflation, and the relationship between these phenomena,
- the state's monetary policy,
- the fiscal policy of the state,
- principles of operation of central and commercial banking, and the financial market,
- principles of operation of the social and economic insurance sector.

Accordingly, it is an environment that affects the level of financial results of enterprises in the short term, and in the long term, on their market value, and thus development opportunities (Kuklińska et al., 2017; Bąk, 2011). It is worth pointing out that the economic environment also shapes the purchasing power of potential customers of enterprises, thus influencing the demand for goods and services.

The functioning of the social environment is largely determined by demographic conditions, including, in particular, the age structure of society, the level of education, birth rate, fertility, and mortality. The shape of this segment of the distal environment is also influenced by less measurable factors, such as: historical or cultural conditions, attitude regarding work, social mobility, religion or family model. Virtual communities associated within social media also play an increasingly important role in the activities of enterprises (Kim, 2021; Hysa et al., 2021;

Zdonek & Król, 2021; Zhang et al., 2009; Parhankangas & Landström, 2006).

In modern economies, the technological environment plays an increasingly important role, which is associated with the progressive digitisation of society and industrial automation (Uygun & Aydin, 2021; Żywiołek et al., 2021; van Dijck, 2020; Dufva & Dufva, 2019; Molenda, 2016). The pace of technological progress is systematically growing, which drives the demand for innovation which is a key factor in socio-economic development. Therefore, among the technological conditions characteristic for the environment of further enterprises, it is worth mentioning:

- access to the latest knowledge and technology, including the speed of transfer and diffusion of knowledge and technology,
- the level of innovation of a given economy,
- the level of public and private financial support for entrepreneurship and innovation,
- the scope and intensity of cooperation between business and science,
- the level of development of start-ups.

Due to the growing climate and raw material problems, the importance of the surrounding environment of enterprises is also growing (Niu & Xiao, 2021; Khojastehpour & Shams, 2020; Xu & Li, 2012). Enterprises must take into account the constraints related to environmental protection, and they must also take actions for an active pro-ecological policy (Janik et al., 2020; Ryszko, 2016). Among factors shaping the functioning of the environmental segment, there are, inter alia:

- the scope and restrictiveness of environmental regulations,
- the adopted raw material policy, including the use of renewable raw materials,
- the knowledge and scale of using the principles of the circular economy,
- the attitude of enterprises to the idea of sustainable development and implementation of the principles of corporate social responsibility (Zdonek et al., 2021),
- the level of eco-innovation development,
- the level of environmental awareness of society and enterprises,

- the level of environmental education.

Due to the growing importance of pro-ecological activities, the costs of carrying them out increase just as with the total costs of enterprises, which significantly affects their financial results (Liu et al., 2020). Therefore, environmental factors are an important determinant of the effectiveness of enterprises and, consequently, the effectiveness of risk management.

The segmentation of the distal environment is closed by the legal environment, which formalises the principles of the functioning of the previously described segments (Li et al., 2021; Yao et al., 2021; Jiao et al., 2015). The legal provisions relating to the activities of enterprises are of a very diverse nature. Among them, it is worth mentioning those concerning:

- the freedom and rules of running a business,
- competition and consumer protection,
- employment and occupational health and safety,
- tax policy,
- the financing of operating and investment activities,
- environmental protection.

They have a direct impact on the income and costs of enterprises, and thus their efficiency. Their scope and restrictiveness also determine the boundaries of the enterprise's operations and the rules of responsibility of its suppliers, recipients, employees and customers. In this way, law and order are shaped, which are also the basis for mutual claims and the protection of business freedoms. The latter issue is also directly related to the principles of the functioning of the judiciary, including: the manner and timely resolution of legal disputes, legal ethics and the scale of corruption in the legal system.

Table 4.2 a summary of this section—presents the potential sources of risk related to individual segments of the distal environment.

To sum up the considerations related to the distal environment, it should be pointed out that due to the already mentioned internationalisation of enterprises and the globalisation of modern economies, it is

Table 4.2 Potential sources of risk related to individual segments of the distal environment

Environment segment	Potential sources of risk
Political	Low marketisation degree of the economy, making it difficult to conduct business. High level of state intervention. High level of public transfers financed from high tax burdens. Closing the economy or a low degree of its internationalisation. Frequent changes of political factions at the government level.
Economic	Economic recession. Low level of economic development. High unemployment and/or inflation. Unfavourable tax system. High level of interest rates and/or restrictive creditworthiness requirements. Lack or low level of development of the financial market limiting access to capital by enterprises. High social security costs for the employer. High costs and/or limited business insurance offer. Low income level of society which adversely affects the demand for goods and services.
Social	Population decline. Ageing of the population, low fertility, high mortality. Reluctance to change, excessive attachment to tradition. Non-consumer life model.
Technological	Low innovativeness of the economy. Poor level of technological knowledge and/or passing on of knowledge and technology. Lack of financial support for innovation by the state and/or private sector. Low level of individual and social entrepreneurship. Low quality of education.

(*continued*)

Table 4.2 (continued)

Environment segment	Potential sources of risk
Environmental	Increased environmental requirements generating additional operating costs. Penalties for violations of environmental restrictions. Low level of environmental awareness and education. Lack of interest and financial support for eco-innovation. Lack of support and understanding of the importance of environmental factors by society, government and enterprises. Lack of knowledge on the principles and benefits of: Circular economy, sustainable development, corporate social responsibility.
Legal	Variation of legal regulations. No or low level of legal regulations in a given area. Over-regulation of the legal system for the business sphere. Corruption in the judicial system. Excessive length of court proceedings.

Source: Own work

currently recommended to conduct an analysis of the distal environment of enterprises not only in the domestic context but also the international context. Additionally, due to the fact that the activities of enterprises are also influenced by local conditions, a separate level of analysis for these factors is proposed. In this way, the postulates of the modified PESTEL analysis are implemented, in the form of: LoNGPESTEL (Local, National, Global, Political, Economic, Social, Technological, Environmental, Legal). Its implementation enables risk tracking in the local, national and international context, which increases the area of threats identyfication and assessment, at the same time contributing to an increase in the effectiveness of risk management.

References

Ansoff, H. I. (2007). *Strategic management*. Palgrave Macmillan.

Ansoff, H. I., Kipley, D., Lewis, A., Helm-Stevens, R., & Ansoff, R. (2019). *Implanting strategic management*. Palgrave Macmillan.

Bąk, M. (2011). Ekonomiczne czynniki otoczenia przedsiębiorstwa a składniki majątku niewidzialnego. *Zeszyty naukowe Uniwersytetu Szczecińskiego, 668*, 23–33.

Bakkar, Y., & Nyola, A. P. (2021). Internationalization, foreign complexity and systemic risk: Evidence from European banks. *Journal of Financial Stability, 55*, 100892.

Banks, E. (2014). *Liquidity risk. Managing funding and asset risk*. Palgrave Macmillan.

Beynon-Davies, P. (2021). *Business analysis and design. Understanding innovation in organisation*. Palgrave Macmillan.

Cvitkovic, E. (1993). *Competition*. Palgrave Macmillan.

Dufva, T., & Dufva, M. (2019). Grasping the future of the digital society. *Futures, 107*, 17–28.

el Namaki, M. S. S. (2014). *Strategic thinking for turbulent times*. Palgrave Macmillan.

Figueira-de-Lemos, F., Johanson, J., & Vahlne, J.-E. (2011). Risk management in the internationalization process of the firm: A note on the Uppsala model. *Journal of World Business, 46*(2), 143–153.

Gaganis, C., Pasiouras, F., & Voulgari, F. (2018). Culture, business environment and SMEs' profitability: Evidence from European countries. *Economic Modelling, 78*, 275–292.

Geisler, E. (2022). *Beyond business analytics. The foundations of behavioral perspective theory*. Palgrave Macmillan.

Hysa, B., Karasek, A., & Zdonek, I. (2021). Social media usage by different generations as a tool for sustainable tourism marketing in Society 5.0 idea. *Sustainability, 12*, 1018.

Janik, A., Ryszko, A., & Szafraniec, M. (2020). Greenhouse gases and circular economy issues in sustainability reports from the energy sector in the European Union. *Energies, 13*(22), 5993.

du Jardin, P. (2021). Dynamic self-organizing feature map-based models applied to bankruptcy prediction. *Decision Support Systems, 147*, 113576.

Jiao, H., Koo, Ch. K, & Cui, Y. (2015). Legal environment, government effectiveness and firms' innovation in China: Examining the moderating influence of government ownership. *Technological Forecasting and Social Change, 96*, 15–24.

Khojastehpour, M., & Shams, S. M. R. (2020). Addressing the complexity of stakeholder management in international ecological setting: A CSR approach. *Journal of Business Research, 119*, 302–309.

Kim, K. H. (2021). Digital and social media marketing in global business environment. *Journal of Business Research, 131*, 627–629.
Kuklińska, E., Masłowski, D., & Dendera-Gruszka, M. (2017). Analiza PEST\PESTEL jako narzędzie wspomagające rozwój miast. Studium przypadku na podstawie miasta Opola. *Zarządzanie Kryzysowe i Bezpieczeństwo, 4*, 155–169.
Li, J., Miao, E., & Zhang, J. (2021). The legal environment, specialized investments, incomplete contracts, and labor productivity. *China Economic Review, 66*, 101583.
Liu, H., Owens, K. A., Yang, K., & Zhang, Ch. (2020). Pollution abatement costs and technical changes under different environmental regulations. *China Economic Review, 62*, 101497.
Molenda, M. (2016). The autonomous maintenance implementation directory as a step toward the intelligent quality management system. *Management Systems in Production Engeenering, 6*(4), 274–279.
Morrison, A., & Roth, K. (1993). Relating Porter's configuration/coordination framework to competitive strategy and structural mechanisms: Analysis and implications. *Journal of Management, 19*(4), 797–818.
Nishihara, M., & Shibata, T. (2020). The effects of asset liquidity on dynamic sell-out and bankruptcy decisions. *European Journal of Operational Research, 288*(3), 1017–1035.
Niu, L., & Xiao, L. (2021). Ecological environment management system based on artificial intelligence and complex numerical optimization. *Microprocessors and Microsystems, 80*, 103627.
Nudurupati, S. S., Garengo, P., & Bititci, U. S. (2021). Impact of the changing business environment on performance measurement and management practices. *International Journal of Production Economics, 232*, 107942.
Parhankangas, A., & Landström, H. (2006). How venture capitalists respond to unmet expectations: The role of social environment. *Journal of Business Venturing, 21*(6), 773–801.
Población García, F. J. (2017). *Financial risk management*. Palgrave Macmillan.
Porter, M. E. (1992). *Strategia konkurencji. Metody analizy sektorów i konkurentów*. Warszawa.
Prajogo, D. I. (2016). The strategic fit between innovation strategies and business environment in delivering business performance. *International Journal of Production Economics, 171*, 241–249.
Romanowska, M. (2015). *Planowanie strategiczne w przedsiębiorstwie*. Warszawa.
Rong, K., & Shi, Y. (2015). *Business ecosystems. constructs, configurations, and the nurturing process*. Palgrave Macmillan.

Rusten, G., & Bryson, J. (Eds.). (2010). *Industrial design, competition and globalization*. Palgrave Macmillan.
Ryszko, A. (2016). Interorganizational cooperation, knowledge sharing and technological eco-innovation: the role of proactive environmental strategy—Empirical evidence from Poland. *Polish Journal of Environmental Studies, 25*(2), 753–763.
Sengupta, J. K. (2004). *Competition and growth*. Palgrave Macmillan.
Stabryła, A. (2000). *Zarządzanie strategiczne w teorii i praktyce firmy*. Warszawa.
Sun, W., Ding, Z., Xu, X., & Cui, K. (2020). Internationalization and firm default risk: The roles of environmental dynamism and marketing capability. *Journal of Business Research, 121*, 142–153.
Uygun, Ö., & Aydin, M. E. (2021). Digital transformation: Industry 4.0 for future minds and future society. *Computers & Industrial Engineering, 157*, 107362.
van Dijck, J. (2020). Governing digital societies: Private platforms, public values. *Computer Law & Security Review, 36*, 105377.
van der Merwe, A. (2015). *Market liquidity risk. Implications for asset pricing, risk management, and financial regulation*. Palgrave Macmillan.
Williamson, D., Jenkins, W., Cooke, P., & Moreton, K. M. (2004). *Strategic management and business analysis*. Elsevier.
Xu, J., & Li, Z. (2012). A review on Ecological Engineering based Engineering Management. *Omega, 40*(3), 368–378.
Yao, J., Xiao, T., & Hou, S. (2021). Risk perceptions and DUI decisions of drivers in different legal environments: New evidence on differential deterrence from a Chinese sample. *Accident Analysis & Prevention, 157*, 106188.
Yunna, W., & Yisheng, Y. (2014). The competition situation analysis of shale gas industry in China: Applying Porter's five forces and scenario model. *Renewable and Sustainable Energy Reviews, 40*, 798–805.
Zdonek, D., & Król, K. (2021). The impact of sex and personality traits on social media use during the COVID-19 pandemic in Poland. *Sustainability, 13*(9), 4793.
Zdonek, I., Mularczyk, A., & Polok, G. (2021). The idea of corporate social responsibility in the opinion of future managers—Comparative research between Poland and Georgia. *Sustainability, 13*(13), 7045.
Zhang, Z., Ilies, R., & Arvey, R. D. (2009). Beyond genetic explanations for leadership: The moderating role of the social environment. *Organizational Behavior and Human Decision Processes, 110*, 118–128.
Żywiołek, J., Molenda, M., & Rosak-Szyroska, J. (2021). Satisfaction with the implementation of Industry 4.0 among manufacturing companies in Poland. *European Research Studies Journal, XXIV*, 592–603.

Rusten, G., & Bryson, J. R. (2010). *Industrial design, competition and globalization*. Palgrave Macmillan.

Ryszko, A. (2016). Interorganizational cooperation, knowledge sharing and technological eco-innovation: the role of proactive environmental strategy—Empirical evidence from Poland. *Polish Journal of Environmental Studies*, [illegible]

S[illegible], J. B. (200[illegible]). *Competition [illegible]*. Palgrave Macmillan.

5

Assessment Model of the Effectiveness of Enterprise Risk Management: A Research Methodology

5.1 Intentions, Stages and Research Model

The considerations presented in Chaps. 1, 2, 3, and 4 are the starting point for developing a research concept and defining a research model. Detailed actions taken in this area are described in this chapter, and then supplemented with the results and conclusions presented in the next two chapters.

The **main purpose** of the research was to identify the determinants of the effectiveness of risk management and to assess the strength of their impact on the degree of achievement of the objectives of risk management (in accordance with the definition of the effectiveness of this process formulated in the first chapter). In this way, the answer to the **key research problem** was sought: What factors affect the effectiveness of risk management and how can they be hierarchised?

To answer the research problem posed, a research plan was developed to achieve the main research goal, as shown in Table 5.1, taking into account: research stages, milestones and specific research methods and tools.

I. Jonek-Kowalska, *Effectiveness of Enterprise Risk Management*,
https://doi.org/10.1007/978-3-030-95376-8_5

Table 5.1 Research plan in the field of determinants of the effectiveness of risk management in the enterprise

Stage	Milestone	Research methods
Identification of potential determinants of the effectiveness of risk management	Selecting and characterising individual groups of determinants of risk management in the enterprise	Literature studies and analysis of research results to date
Development of a research model	Determining possible cause and effect relationships between groups of determinants and the effectiveness of risk management.	Modelling of economic processes and phenomena.
Designing a research tool	Translating the model assumptions into a set of questions addressed to enterprises.	Questionnaire.
Selection of a research sample	Statistical determination of the sample size to ensure that it is representative.	The formula for the size of a sample representative for a finite population and the stratified selection method.
Initial analysis of research results	Obtaining basic statistical information on risk management in the surveyed enterprises.	Descriptive statistics tools and methods (Statistica package).
In-depth analysis of research results	Examination of the strengths and the direction of multidimensional dependencies in the developed research model.	Modelling of structural equations.
Formulating results and practical recommendations	Confrontation of the research results with the current theoretical and practical observations. Development of recommendations for the improvement of risk management in practice.	Comparative analysis as well as deduction and reduction.

Source: Own work

As already mentioned, the introductory, theoretical chapters of this monograph were literature studies in the field of risk management and the effectiveness of this process. On their basis, four groups of determinants of the effectiveness of risk management in the enterprise were selected, which include:

1. behavioural factors, such as: risk perception, propensity and attitudes, integrally related to human resources, primarily including managers and persons responsible for risk in the enterprise;
2. methodological factors related to the selection of risk management methods and techniques, their scope and the diligence with which they are used;
3. resource factors relating to resources used in the risk management process, in particular human and financial resources;
4. factors related to the internal and external environment (proximal and distal environment), which are a source of multifaceted and complex threats for the enterprise.

The above groups mentioned were included in the structure of the research model presented in Fig. 5.2.

This model assumes that all selected groups of factors affect the effectiveness of risk management in the enterprise. Additionally, it was assumed that the relations will be verified between:

- behavioural factors and methodological factors in the search for the relationship between the management's perception of risk and the scope of risk mitigation instruments selected by them;
- behavioural and resource factors in order to identify the impact of psychosocial variables on the involvement of human and financial resources in the risk management process in the enterprise;
- factors related to the proximal and more distal environment and methodological factors aimed at determining whether the scope of threats affects the scope of protection against the risk;
- factors related to the proximal and distal environment and resource factors, which will allow to determine whether the scope of threats affects the involvement of resources in the risk management process in the enterprise.

The research model presented in Fig. 5.1, developed on the basis of literature assumptions, has been detailed and operationalised in the form of a questionnaire. Its verification was carried out with the use of descriptive statistics and structural equation modelling tools. The calculations were made using the *Statistica* package. The results of these stages are presented later in this monograph.

5.2 Operationalisation of the Research Model in the Form of a Questionnaire

The questionnaire operationalising the research model consisted of four parts relating to the individual factors determining the effectiveness of risk management and the dimensions of assessing the effectiveness of risk management in the enterprise as a dependent variable. The respondents referred to all statements formulated in the questionnaire using the five point Likert scale.

Thus, Table 5.2 presents a set of questions regarding behavioural factors.

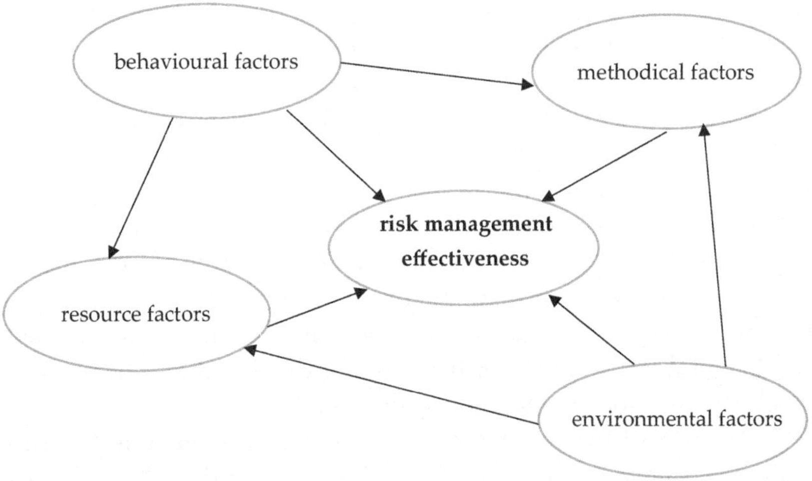

Fig. 5.1 General structure of the adopted research model. (Source: Own work)

Table 5.2 Descriptive variables for behavioural factors (BH)

Series	Descriptive variable	Assignment to a group of determinants
BH1	In an enterprise, risk is primarily associated with threats.	Risk perception
BH2	Managers do not like and do not want to take risks.	Tendency to take risks
BH3	The enterprise tries to avoid risky ventures.	Attitudes towards risk
BH4	Managers are primarily concerned with internal threats.	Attitudes towards risk
BH5	Managers are primarily concerned with external threats.	Attitudes towards risk

Assessment scale: (1) Does not apply to my enterprise. (2) Applies to my enterprise to a small extent. (3) Partially applies to my enterprise. (4) Applies to my enterprise to a significant extent. (5) Fully applies to my enterprise
Source: Own work

The behavioural factors were identified using the parameters described in the second chapter. The first statement made it possible to determine how much risk is associated with threats, which in turn made it possible to determine the way risk was perceived. The second statement allowed to assess the tendency to take risks (Wodarski, 2021). Next, three subsequent statements identified attitudes towards risk in terms of: general and in relation to internal and external threats, respectively (Kowalska-Styczeń, 2016, 2020; Jonek-Kowalska & Wawiernia, 2016).

The second group of determinants related to the methodology of risk management in the enterprise and covered the questions contained in Table 5.3.

The statements in Table 5.3 allowed to determine the scope of risk management determined by the subsequent stages of this process, including: threats identyfication, assessment, mitigation and control (Hofman et al., 2017; Nawrocki & Jonek-Kowalska, 2016a, b; Bijańska & Wodarski, 2014). They also made it possible to identify the most frequently used methods of risk management, taking into account their division into the previously described material control (avoidance / prevention) and financial control (risk transfer / risk retention). Additionally, within the described group, the statements referring to detailed, typical

Table 5.3 Descriptive variables for risk management (RM)

Series	Descriptive variable	Assignment to a group of determinants
RM1	The enterprise identifies and describes the sources of risk.	Risk management steps: identification
RM2	In the enterprise, losses related to the occurrence of risk and the possibility of their occurrence are estimated.	Risk management steps: assessment
RM3	The enterprise does not ignore potential sources of risk.	Risk management: material control—avoidance
RM4	The enterprise uses various forms of prevention to prevent the occurrence of risk.	Risk management: material control—prevention
RM5	The enterprise uses business insurance whenever possible.	Risk management: financial control—risk transfer
RM6	Apart from business insurance, the enterprise also uses other paid forms of protection against risk, e.g. futures contracts.	Risk management: financial control—risk transfer
RM7	As part of hedging against risk, the enterprise establishes various forms of cooperation with other enterprises and / or institutions.	Risk management: financial control—risk transfer
RM8	The enterprise accepts the necessity to finance the risk transfer (e.g. insurance) and does not avoid it.	Risk management: financial control—risk retention
RM9	The enterprise carries out risk control.	Risk management steps: risk control

Assessment scale: (1) Does not apply to my enterprise. (2) Applies to my enterprise to a small extent. (3) Partially applies to my enterprise. (4) Applies to my enterprise to a significant extent. (5) Fully applies to my enterprise

Source: Own work

methods of financial risk control, such as: insurance, economic cooperation or futures contracts, were made more precise.

The model also takes into account the resource conditions characterised in theoretical terms in the third chapter. In research terms, they are presented in Table 5.4.

Statements regarding resource factors allowed to determine whether in the risk management process the enterprise only uses its own resources or uses external assistance. They also made it possible to assess the

Table 5.4 Descriptive variables for resources involved in risk management (RES)

Series	Descriptive variable	Assignment to a group of determinants
RES1	The enterprise employs experts in the field of risk management.	Own human resources: internal experts.
RES2	There is a department dealing with risk management in the enterprise.	Own organisational resources: a department in the organisational structure.
RES3	The enterprise involves all employees in the risk management process.	Own human resources: employee participation in risk management.
RES4	The enterprise uses its own internal risk management systems.	Own organisational resources: internal risk management system.
RES5	The enterprise uses an advanced risk management system developed by an external entity.	External organisational and human resources: an advanced risk management system developed by external experts.

Assessment scale: (1) Does not apply to my enterprise. (2) Applies to my enterprise to a small extent. (3) Partially applies to my enterprise. (4) Applies to my enterprise to a significant extent. (5) Fully applies to my enterprise

Source: Own work

advancement of the risk management process. The least advanced approach to risk management is the sole use of own specialists without separating the department performing tasks in the area of risk mitigation. An internal department dealing with risk reduction activities is a higher level. And the highest level of advancement is represented by holistic risk management systems (Jonek-Kowalska & Nawrocki, 2019), the so-called *Enterprise Risk Management (ERM)*.

As part of resource questions, the scale of employee involvement in risk management was also assessed, because—as pointed out in Chap. 3—employee participation is an important determinant of the effectiveness of risk management in an enterprise. Employees are a valuable source of information on risk sources, and participation in management allows them to identify with the company and increase their involvement in work and risk mitigation activities.

Indirectly, questions about the involvement of human and organisational resources also allow to determine the enterprise's financial expenditure on risk management. As the advancement of the risk management process increases, the expenses and costs of creating and maintaining such systems increase.

The last group of determinants concerned the risk exposure that related to the internal, proximal and distal environment. Statements allowing to determine their individual strength are presented in Table 5.5.

The questions concerning the environment of the enterprise focus on the factors constituting the source of the most serious economic threats. The following were recognised as such: loss of financial liquidity and lack of funds for business operations. Both of the above mentioned threats directly affect the interior of the enterprise, however, as already mentioned, they are also related to the proximal and distal environment,

Table 5.5 Descriptive variables for the risk exposure that related to the internal, proximal and distal environment (ENV)

Series	Descriptive variable	Assignment to a group of determinants
ENV1	The most serious threats arise inside the enterprise.	The interior of the enterprise.
ENV2	The most serious internal source of risk is human resources.	The interior of the enterprise.
ENV3	The most serious internal source of risk is the lack of financial liquidity.	The interior of the enterprise.
ENV4	The most serious internal source of risk is the lack of funds.	The interior and distal environment of enterprises.
ENV5	The relationships with suppliers are the most intense source of risk in an enterprise.	Proximal environment: suppliers.
ENV6	Relations with recipients are the most intense source of risk in an enterprise.	Proximal environment: recipients.
ENV7	The greatest source of risk is the enterprise's competition.	Proximal environment: competition.
ENV8	The enterprise is very sensitive to economic fluctuations.	Distal environment.
EN9	Changes in the international environment have a strong impact on the enterprise's operations.	Distal environment.

Assessment scale: (1) Does not apply to my enterprise. (2) Applies to my enterprise to a small extent. (3) Partially applies to my enterprise. (4) Applies to my enterprise to a significant extent. (5) Fully applies to my enterprise

Source: Own work

primarily including customers (being the source of financial profits) and the financial market (being the source of equity and / or foreign capital). Many internal threats also arise as a result of human negligence and errors, and therefore they were included in the detailed research questions.

In the case of the proximal environment, the statements made in the questionnaire concerned the most important forces of Porter, that is: recipients, suppliers and competitors. Analysis of the distal environment focuses on changes in the economic situation—which have always been significant and have a strong impact on enterprises (Jonek-Kowalska, 2019)—and on the international segment, which in the twenty-first century became one of the key business determinants thanks to globalisation and internationalisation (Nawrocki & Jonek-Kowalska, 2016; Jonek-Kowalska, 2017).

The questionnaire also included statements about the dependent variable, i.e. the effectiveness of risk management in the enterprise. Their content is presented in Table 5.6.

The efficiency statements are divided into three perspectives. The first one arises from the definition of risk management effectiveness formulated in the first chapter. According to this definition, risk management is effective if it protects the enterprise against threats and losses. In the short term, this should support the process of the enterprise's survival on the market, and in the long term it should enable a fairly undisturbed development (Jonek-Kowalska, 2015).

Table 5.6 Descriptive variables for assessing the effectiveness of risk management

Series	Descriptive variable	Perspective
EF1	Risk management in the enterprise minimises risks and losses.	Definitive, directly related to the definition of risk management effectiveness.
EF2	Risk management in the enterprise enables survival in the market.	Short term, current, focused on operational goals.
EF3	Risk management supports the development of the enterprise.	Long term, focused on strategic goals.

Assessment scale: (1) Does not apply to my enterprise. (2) Applies to my enterprise to a small extent. (3) Partially applies to my enterprise. (4) Applies to my enterprise to a significant extent. (5) Fully applies to my enterprise

Source: Own work

5.3 Selection and Characteristics of the Research Sample

Research on the effectiveness of risk management was carried out on a representative research sample of Polish enterprises. The sample only included medium and large-sized enterprises due to the lack of advanced methods and risk management systems in small-sized enterprises. In the sampling process, a 95% confidence level and a 5% maximum error were assumed at the fraction size of 0.5. With the above assumptions, the sample size included 722 enterprises, taking into account the stratified selection for two criteria:

1. organisations divided into medium and large-sized enterprises,
2. organisations divided by economy sector: production, trade, services and construction.

Characteristics of the sample composition taking into account the above criteria are presented in Figs. 5.2 and 5.3.

The period of enterprise operation on the market was also included in the questionnaire data. The division of the respondents considering this criterion is shown in Fig. 5.4.

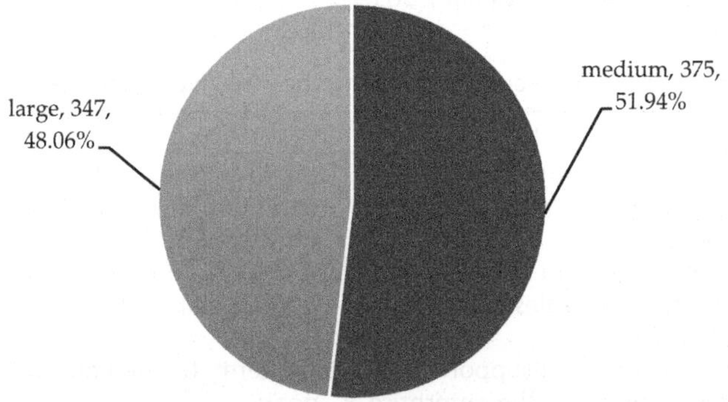

Fig. 5.2 The structure of the research sample in terms of the size of the enterprise expressed in the number of employees (50–249: medium-sized enterprise; 250 and more: large-sized enterprise—consistent with the structure of the Polish economy). (Source: Own work)

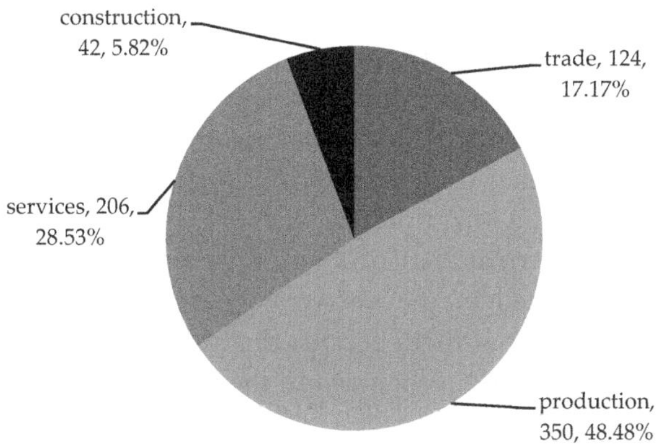

Fig. 5.3 Structure of the research sample considering sectoral affiliation (production; trade; services; construction—consistent with the structure of the Polish economy). (Source: Own work)

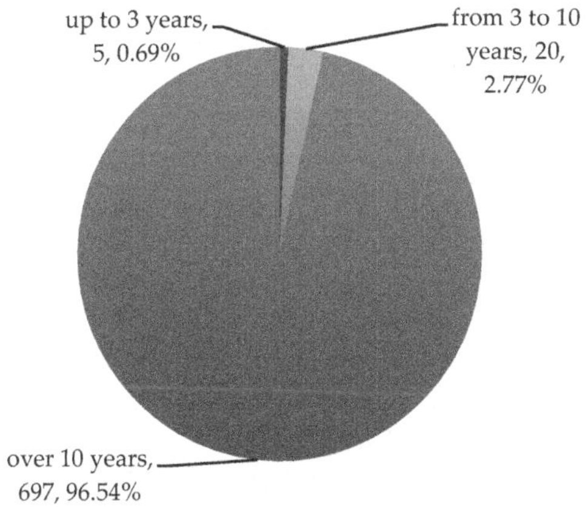

Fig. 5.4 The structure of the research sample considering the period of running a business. (Source: Own work)

According to the data presented in Fig. 5.4, the vast majority of surveyed enterprises are entities with extensive market experience, operating for over 10 years. The selection of enterprises in this aspect is not representative and is intentional. Knowing the risks requires a long history of experiences that have been felt by mature companies that have dealt with threats for a long time.

The results of the research carried out in the research sample defined in this way are presented in the next two chapters of this monograph. Conclusions arising from them became the basis for formulating recommendations and suggestions included in the last part of the book.

References

Bijańska, J., & Wodarski, K. (2014). Risk management in the planning of development projects in the industrial enterprises. *Metalurgija, 53*(2), 276–278.

Hofman, M., Spałek, S., & Grela, G. (2017). Shedding new light on project portfolio risk management. *Sustainability, 9*(10), 1798.

Jonek-Kowalska, I. (2015). Risk, profitability and value of the leading steel producers on the world capital markets. *Metalurgija, 54*(1), 273–275.

Jonek-Kowalska, I. (2017). How do turbulent sectoral conditions sector influence the value of coal mining enterprises? Perspectives from the Central-Eastern Europe coal mining industry. *Resources Policy, 55*, 103–122.

Jonek-Kowalska, I. (2019). Exposure of Polish enterprises to risk within business cycle. *Managerial Economics, 19*(2), 187–203.

Jonek-Kowalska, I., & Nawrocki, T. (2019). Holistic fuzzy evaluation of operational risk in Polish mining enterprises in a long-term and sectoral research perspective. *Resources Policy, 63*, 1–11.

Jonek-Kowalska, I., & Wawiernia, A. (2016). How do Polish managers perceive and manage risk? Experience from the Silesian region. *Proceedings of the 12th European Conference on Management, Leadership and Governance ECMLG 2016*, November 10–11, 2016, Bucharest, Romania. Pinzaru Florina, Bratianu Constantin, 116–124.

Kowalska-Styczeń, A. (2016). Study of social organizational processes in the context of complex systems. Research advancements in national and global business. Theory and practice. *11th Annual Conference of the EuroMed Academy of Business*, September 12–14, 2018, Valletta, Malta. Conference readings. Book proceedings. Ed. Demetris Vrontis, Yaakov Weber, Evangelos Tsoukatos. EuroMed Press, 818–833.

Kowalska-Styczeń, A. (2020). How to study complex social phenomena in the organization? Education excellence and innovation management: A 2025 vision to sustain economic development during global challenges. *Proceedings of the 35th International Business Information Management Association Conference (IBIMA)*, April 1–2, 2020, Seville, Spain. Ed. Khalid S. Soliman. International Business Information Management Association, 5194–5205.

Nawrocki, T., & Jonek-Kowalska, I. (2016a). Assessing operational risk in coal mining enterprises – Internal, industrial and international perspectives. *Resources Policy, 48*, 5–67.

Nawrocki, T., & Jonek-Kowalska, I. (2016b). Fuzzy logic in risk assesment of a mining enterprise in the context of Polish economic conditions. *Zeszyty Naukowe Politechniki Śląskiej, seria: Organizacja i Zarządzanie, 81*, 49–65.

Wodarski, K. (2021). *Management and decision making methods. Theoretical and practical aspects.* Wydawictwo Naukowe TYGIEL.

6

Determinants of Risk Management Effectiveness: Preliminary Analysis of Research Results from Polish Enterprises

6.1 Behavioural and Methodical Determinants of the Effectiveness of Risk Management

Personality traits of managers and their individual set of experiences affect the decision making process in the enterprise, and therefore:

- risk perception,
- tendency to take risks,
- and attitudes towards risk may determine the effectiveness of risk management.

For these reasons, the above mentioned variables were taken into account in the course of the survey. Table 6.1 presents the obtained results relating to the behavioural factors characterising Polish managers in medium and large-sized enterprises. Table 6.2 presents descriptive statistics for the characterised determinant group.

The first question in the survey related to the perception of risk. Thus, in light of the results presented in Table 6.1, it can be concluded that

I. Jonek-Kowalska, *Effectiveness of Enterprise Risk Management*,
https://doi.org/10.1007/978-3-030-95376-8_6

Table 6.1 Responses for behavioural factors (BH)

Series	Descriptive variable	1	2	3	4	5
BH1	In an enterprise, risk is primarily associated with threats.	65 9.00%	158 21.88%	299 41.41%	154 21.33%	46 6.37%
BH2	Managers do not like and do not want to take risks.	146 20.22%	227 31.44%	239 33.10%	90 12.47%	20 2.77%
BH3	The enterprise tries to avoid risky ventures.	89 12.33%	187 25.90%	192 26.59%	173 23.96%	81 11.22%
BH4	Managers are primarily concerned with internal threats.	150 20.78%	277 38.37%	212 29.36%	67 9.28%	16 2.22%
BH5	Managers are primarily concerned with external threats.	67 9.28%	133 18.42%	239 33.10%	216 29.92%	67 9.28%

Assessment scale: (1) Does not apply to my enterprise. (2) Applies to my enterprise to a small extent. (3) Partially applies to my enterprise. (4) Applies to my enterprise to a significant extent. (5) Fully applies to my enterprise

Source: Own work

Polish managers do not only perceive risk as a threat. Most of the respondents believe that such a negative view applies only partially, to a small extent or not at all, to the entity they manage. The value of the upper quartile, amounting to 4.00, shows that 75% of the surveyed Polish entrepreneurs have a positive or neutral view of risk. It should also be added that the respondents are quite unanimous in their opinions, which is confirmed by the lowest value of the coefficient of variation in the group of analysed factors.

Such a distribution of responses indicates that the risk in Polish enterprises is also perceived as a chance for success and additional benefits. The identified approach—in line with the considerations presented in the theoretical part—is characterised by people who are entrepreneurial, active, willing to act and not afraid of new challenges. It fosters innovation and development. However, it is worth adding that a significant or complete failure to perceive risk in the context of threats may be associated with ignoring its existence and downplaying its effects, and this in turn will not be conducive to the effectiveness of risk management.

The second question in the group of behavioural factors was to identify the tendency to take risks. The answers provided show that Polish

Table 6.2 Responses for behavioural factors (BEH)

Series	Average	Median	Mode	Mode size	Lower quartile	Upper quartile	Standard deviation	Coefficient of variation (%)	Skewness	Kurtosis
BEH1	2.94	3.00	3.00	299.00	2.00	4.00	1.02	34.75	-0.03	-0.37
BEH2	2.46	2.00	3.00	239.00	2.00	3.00	1.03	42.03	0.27	-0.53
BEH3	2.96	3.00	3.00	192.00	2.00	4.00	1.20	40.57	0.04	-0.94
BEH4	2.34	2.00	2.00	277.00	2.00	3.00	0.98	41.89	0.45	-0.22
BEH5	3.11	3.00	3.00	239.00	2.00	4.00	1.10	35.38	-0.23	-0.62

Key:
BEH1: In an enterprise, risk is primarily associated with threats
BEH2: Managers do not like and do not want to take risks
BEH3: The enterprise tries to avoid risky ventures
BEH4: Managers are primarily concerned with internal threats
BEH5: Managers are primarily concerned with external threats
Assessment scale: (1) Does not apply to my enterprise. (2) Applies to my enterprise to a small extent. (3) Partially applies to my enterprise. (4) Applies to my enterprise to a significant extent. (5) Fully applies to my enterprise
Source: Own work

managers like taking risk and are not afraid of it, which corresponds to and most likely results from a positive perception of this phenomenon. The value of the mode, amounting to 3.00, and the right-skewed distribution of answers indicate that the vast majority of respondents declare their willingness and readiness to take risks. In practice, this means efficient decision making without fear and anxiety related to the potential threats that accompany them. However, it is worth adding that the identification of tendencies to take risk is accompanied by the greatest variability of responses, which proves the diversity of the attitudes characterised. This differentiation may result from a different history of experiences, it may also be related to the personality traits of decision makers. However, it is not related to the period of operation on the market, because the group of surveyed enterprises mainly includes entities that have been running a business for over 10 years (over 96% of respondents).

In the next question on behavioural factors, respondent attitudes towards risk were assessed, which include:

- taking risk (active attitude),
- ignoring risk (indifferent attitude),
- avoiding risk (passive attitude).

The high values of the mode and the upper quartile let us state that despite the positive perception of risk and high tendencies to take risk, Polish enterprises do not want to engage in risky ventures that could be a source of above average benefits for them. In such a situation, most of them show a conservative attitude and prefer to avoid risk.

Such a distribution of responses suggests a certain subjectivity and declaration of the perception of risk and the tendencies to take risk. It can also testify to the prudence and attentiveness of managers who do not want to expose the enterprise's operations to excessive risk and expose it to the possibility of suffering significant damage and losses (Jonek-Kowalska, 2020a).

The last two questions in the part of the questionnaire relating to behavioural factors concerned the level of fear of internal and external threats and constituted a general introduction to the questions about the enterprise's environment. The responses obtained in this regard show that external threats raise much greater concern among the surveyed enterprises. This is confirmed by the value of the mode, which:

- for internal threats is 2.00 and means that the fear of internal threats concerns the surveyed enterprises to a small extent,
- and for external threats it is 3.00 and it means that the fear of external threats concerns the respondents to a greater extent.

The above conclusion is also reflected in the opposite skews of the response distribution, right-skewed for internal threats and left-skewed for external threats, and a higher value of the upper quartile for external risk sources (4.00). It should also be pointed out that the respondents are more unanimous in the assessment of the significance of external threats than internal threats, as proven by the lower values of the coefficient of variation for the former. Therefore, among the surveyed enterprises there are also those where internal sources of risk may pose a serious threat to the functioning of the enterprise (over 11% of respondents for which the internal risk was assessed at 4.00 and 5.00).

The assessment of behavioural factors shows that a positive perception of risk prevails in the surveyed enterprises. Managers tend to like risks and are not afraid to take them. Nevertheless, in the case of risky situations, they prefer to be conservative, fearing serious damage and loss. At the same time, they feel more anxious in the case of external threats, being much less afraid of internal sources of risk.

The second group of risk management effectiveness determinants identified on the basis of literature studies were methodological factors relating to the risk management process and tools in the enterprise. These research results are presented in Tables 6.3 and 6.4.

The first and second questions included in the survey related to the two initial stages of risk management, which determined the further course of this process and its effectiveness. These stages include identification of risk sources and assessment of the effects of potential threats in the form of estimating damage and losses. Their main task is to make decision makers aware of the intensity and scale of possible threats. Lack of or errors in carrying out these stages result in the inappropriate selection of

Table 6.3 Responses for methodological factors (RM)

Series	Descriptive variable	1	2	3	4	5
RM1	The enterprise identifies and describes the sources of risk.	75 10.39%	98 13.57%	207 28.67%	187 25.90%	155 21.47%
RM2	In the enterprise, losses related to the occurrence of risk and the possibility of their occurrence are estimated.	56 7.76%	145 20.08%	215 29.78%	185 25.62%	121 16.76%
RM3	The enterprise does not ignore potential sources of risk.	18 2.49%	70 9.70%	161 22.30%	263 36.43%	210 29.09%
RM4	The enterprise uses various forms of prevention to prevent the occurrence of risk.	29 4.02%	88 12.19%	190 26.32%	259 35.87%	156 21.61%
RM5	The enterprise uses business insurance whenever possible.	64 8.86%	68 9.42%	158 21.88%	234 32.41%	198 27.42%
RM6	Apart from business insurance, the enterprise also uses other paid forms of protection against risk, e.g. futures contracts.	157 21.75%	110 15.24%	167 23.13%	183 25.35%	105 14.54%
RM7	As part of hedging against risk, the enterprise establishes various forms of cooperation with other enterprises and / or institutions.	91 12.60%	142 19.67%	214 29.64%	188 26.04%	87 12.05%
RM8	The enterprise accepts the necessity to finance the risk transfer (e.g. insurance) and does not avoid it.	89 12.33%	114 15.79%	213 29.50%	185 25.62%	121 16.76%
RM9	The enterprise carries out risk control.	63 8.73%	96 13.30%	210 29.09%	201 27.84%	152 21.05%

Assessment scale: (1) Does not apply to my enterprise. (2) Applies to my enterprise to a small extent. (3) Partially applies to my enterprise. (4) Applies to my enterprise to a significant extent. (5) Fully applies to my enterprise

Source: Own work

Table 6.4 Responses for methodological factors (RM)

Series	Average	Median	Mode	Mode size	Lower quartile	Upper quartile	Standard deviation	Coefficient of variation (%)	Skewness	Kurtosis
RM1	3.34	3.00	3.00	207.00	3.00	4.00	1.25	37.25	-0.33	-0.81
RM2	3.24	3.00	3.00	215.00	2.00	4.00	1.18	36.36	-0.13	-0.84
RM3	3.80	4.00	4.00	263.00	3.00	5.00	1.04	27.45	-0.64	-0.24
RM4	3.59	4.00	4.00	259.00	3.00	4.00	1.08	30.02	-0.49	-0.40
RM5	3.60	4.00	4.00	234.00	3.00	5.00	1.23	34.13	-0.66	-0.46
RM6	2.96	3.00	4.00	183.00	2.00	4.00	1.36	46.10	-0.09	-1.21
RM7	3.05	3.00	3.00	214.00	2.00	4.00	1.20	39.34	-0.12	-0.87
RM8	3.19	3.00	3.00	213.00	2.00	4.00	1.24	39.00	-0.22	-0.87
RM9	3.39	3.00	3.00	210.00	3.00	4.00	1.20	35.51	-0.36	-0.71

Key:
RM1: The enterprise identifies and describes the sources of risk
RM2: In the enterprise, losses related to the occurrence of risk and the possibility of their occurrence are estimated
RM3: The enterprise does not ignore potential sources of risk
RM4: The enterprise uses various forms of prevention to prevent the occurrence of risk
RM5: The enterprise uses business insurance whenever possible
RM6: Apart from business insurance, the enterprise also uses other paid forms of protection against risk, e.g. futures contracts
RM7: As part of hedging against risk, the enterprise establishes various forms of cooperation with other enterprises and / or institutions
RM8: The enterprise accepts the necessity to finance the risk transfer (e.g. insurance) and does not avoid it
RM9: The enterprise carries out risk control
Assessment scale: (1) Does not apply to my enterprise. (2) Applies to my enterprise to a small extent. (3) Partially applies to my enterprise. (4) Applies to my enterprise to a significant extent. (5) Fully applies to my enterprise
Source: Own work

risk mitigation tools and / or insufficient protection against threats, which in turn may reduce the effectiveness of risk management and expose the enterprise to excessive threats.

The obtained responses show that the vast majority of surveyed enterprises identify and describe the sources of risk. Nevertheless, around 24% of respondents say that this stage of risk management does not apply to their enterprise or at least only to a limited extent. This means that a quarter of Polish medium and large-sized enterprises do not know what risks they may face and what losses they may cause in the course of their operations.

Over 27% of the surveyed enterprises do not carry out a risk assessment or carry one out to a small extent. In this context, there are also significantly fewer answers of the respondents confirming that the risk assessment fully applies to their enterprise. This means that the identification stage is not continued and deepened, and some enterprises that identified the risk no longer assess it. This is confirmed by the lower value of the arithmetic mean and the lower quartile compared to the values of these parameters for threats identification.

However, it should be pointed out that a significant part of the surveyed medium and large-sized enterprises (about ¾) both identifies and assesses the risk, which is confirmed by the close number of individual responses to the first two survey questions and a similar left-skewed value for the distribution of these responses. Lower number of enterprises assessing the risk is reflected in a lower value of kurtosis indicating a greater flattening of the distribution.

Statements from 3 to 7 in the part concerning methodological factors referred to the methods of risk mitigation, among which material and financial control were distinguished in the theoretical part. The material control includes: risk avoidance and prevention, and financial control: risk transfer and risk retention. Thus, in the case of the statement relating to risk avoidance (citing: *The enterprise does not ignore potential sources of risk*) only 12% of the surveyed enterprises replied that they did not apply at all or applied to a small extent to their methods of mitigating risks. Therefore, the vast majority of respondents initially declared an active attitude focused on limiting the risks and their possible effects, which is confirmed by the high value of the arithmetic mean, the high value of the lower quartile (3.00) and the maximum value of the upper quartile (5.00). It should also be added that the surveyed enterprises are quite consistent in terms of a serious approach to the identified risks, because the distribution of assessments for this statement is characterised by the lowest coefficient of variation in the group of methodological factors.

Included in a further part of the questionnaire are in-depth statements aimed at identifying the forms of risk mitigation used as part of the material and financial control. Figure 6.1 synthetically presents the forms that the surveyed enterprises indicated most often (sum of responses regarding the following statements: (4) Applies to my enterprise to a significant extent and (5) Fully applies to my enterprise for RM4–RM7 factors).

The data presented in Fig. 6.1 shows that the surveyed enterprises most often use economic insurance as a financial method of risk mitigation. Prevention as a typical form of material risk control is slightly less popular. A significant proportion of the respondents also use other forms of risk transfer for a fee (e.g. derivatives) and establish economic cooperation with other market entities in order to mitigate risks.

The obtained results prove that Polish enterprises know and use various risk management methods and tools. Nevertheless, these are the most common and widely available methods. Although their use entails

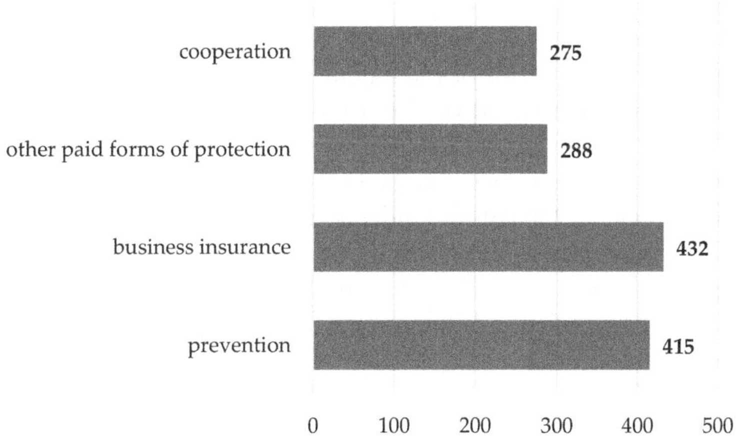

Fig. 6.1 Methods of risk mitigation most often used in the surveyed enterprises. (Source: Own work)

additional costs, most enterprises behave rationally and prefer a fee in return for avoiding serious damage and risks. Therefore, it can be concluded that risk transfer is considered a convenient, effective and efficient way to reduce economic risk (Jonek-Kowalska, 2020b).

In the group of surveyed enterprises, and therefore also in the wider economic reality, there are actually about 16–17% of enterprises (sum of responses regarding the following statements: (1) Does not apply to my enterprise and (2) Applies to my enterprise to a small extent in the case of RM4 and RM5 factors), which practically do not use any risk management methods, as neither economic insurance nor prevention apply to them. This group increases to around 32%–35% in the case of the sum of indications relating to other forms of risk transfer (RM6 factor) and economic cooperation as a method of risk mitigation (RM7 factor).

This may be because threats are ignored and, as a result, risk is avoided. Such an attitude to risk may also result from the difficult financial situation and the lack of funds to pay for the risk transfer and preventive measures, which in turn refers to the conscious risk retention described in the theoretical part as one of the possible but not recommended forms of risk mitigation. Regardless of the reason for the lack of hedging against risk, it should be pointed out that a passive attitude towards threats exposes the enterprise to serious consequences of risk implementation in the form of damages and losses that may threaten the continuity of the enterprise's operations and even lead to bankruptcy.

The assessment analysis of the statement relating to the acceptance of the fee for risk transfer (RM8 factor) allows the presumption that the main reason for the lack of hedging against risk in the above described minority group of enterprises is the lack or insufficient level of financial resources. Around 28% of respondents state that they avoid fees for risk transfer (sum of responses regarding the following statements: (1) Does not apply to my enterprise and (2) Applies to my enterprise to a small extent in the case of the RM8 factor), which partially coincides with the number of indications regarding the lack of business insurance and risk prevention. However, the vast majority of Polish medium and large-sized enterprises agree to finance the risk transfer, which confirms the previous conclusions resulting from the identification and assessment of the scale of the use of risk management tools.

Most of the surveyed enterprises also carry out a risk management audit, which is the last step in this process. Only about 22% of enterprises declare that the control activities do not apply to them or apply to them to a small extent. This lets us conclude that in the vast majority of Polish enterprises, the risk management process takes into account all stages necessary for its continuity and effectiveness, that is: threats identification, assessment, mitigation and control.

The assessment analysis of methodological factors shows that the majority of Polish medium and large-sized enterprises know and apply risk management procedures. This process is carried out in accordance with theoretical recommendations and includes four necessary steps. As part of risk mitigation, enterprises primarily use economic insurance and anti-risk prevention, which is quite a typical and convenient solution. Some of them extend protection to other risk transfer instruments and economic cooperation, which bodes well for increasing the effectiveness of risk management. The group of about 15%–20% of enterprises that do not take measures to reduce risk, do not identify it, do not evaluate it and do not make efforts to mitigate it should be assessed negatively. This makes them vulnerable to above average risks and losses.

In the further part of the monograph, the analysis of methodological factors will be deepened by the resource approach, which also allows to learn about the qualitative determinants of the risk management process in Polish small and medium-sized enterprises.

6.2 Resource and Environmental Determinants of the Effectiveness of Risk Management

As already mentioned, another group of determinants of the effectiveness of risk management in an enterprise includes resource factors, including human and organisational resources, and indirectly—in the context of the advancement of the risk management systems used—also financial resources. The assessment results of individual statements concerning resource factors are presented in Tables 6.5 and 6.6.

Table 6.5 Responses for resource factors (RES)

Series	Descriptive variable	1	2	3	4	5
RES1	The enterprise employs experts in the field of risk management.	370 51.25%	118 16.34%	98 13.57%	80 11.08%	56 7.76%
RES2	There is a department dealing with risk management in the enterprise.	396 54.85%	107 14.82%	93 12.88%	56 7.76%	70 9.70%
RES3	The enterprise involves all employees in the risk management process.	146 20.22%	172 23.82%	193 26.73%	132 18.28%	79 10.94%
RES4	The enterprise uses its own internal risk management systems.	116 16.07%	132 18.28%	177 24.52%	175 24.24%	122 16.90%
RES5	The enterprise uses an advanced risk management system developed by an external entity.	468 64.82%	82 11.36%	83 11.50%	63 8.73%	26 3.60%

Assessment scale: (1) Does not apply to my enterprise. (2) Applies to my enterprise to a small extent. (3) Partially applies to my enterprise. (4) Applies to my enterprise to a significant extent. (5) Fully applies to my enterprise
Source: Own work

The resource factors were assessed as the worst among the determinants analysed so far, as proved by very low values of the arithmetic mean and the mode. This means that the surveyed enterprises are aiming towards minimising the costs associated with risk management and, admittedly, engage in this process, but mainly with the use of human, organisational and financial resources gathered so far. In the context of this initial reflection, the detailed responses of the respondents are analysed below.

Thus, only about 19% of the surveyed medium and large-sized enterprises employ experts in the field of risk management (sum of responses to the following statements: (4) Applies to my enterprise to a significant extent and (5) Fully applies to my enterprise for the RES1 factor), which means that companies mainly use their own managerial resources, not necessarily specialised in the field of risk management in enterprises. The minimum value of the median of 1.00 confirms this conclusion because

Table 6.6 Responses for resource factors (RES)

Series	Average	Median	Mode	Mode size	Lower quartile	Upper quartile	Standard deviation	Coefficient of variation (%)	Skewness	Kurtosis
RES1	2.08	1.00	1.00	370.00	1.00	3.00	1.34	64.32	0.92	-0.49
RES2	2.03	1.00	1.00	396.00	1.00	3.00	1.36	67.34	1.06	-0.25
RES3	2.76	3.00	3.00	193.00	2.00	4.00	1.27	46.01	0.19	-0.99
RES4	3.08	3.00	3.00	177.00	2.00	4.00	1.32	42.89	-0.12	-1.11
RES5	1.75	1.00	1.00	468.00	1.00	2.00	1.17	67.04	1.36	0.59

Key:
RES1: The enterprise employs experts in the field of risk management
RES2: There is a department dealing with risk management in the enterprise
RES3: The enterprise involves all employees in the risk management process
RES4: The enterprise uses its own internal risk management systems
RES5: The enterprise uses an advanced risk management system developed by an external entity
Assessment scale: (1) Does not apply to my enterprise. (2) Applies to my enterprise to a small extent. (3) Partially applies to my enterprise. (4) Applies to my enterprise to a significant extent. (5) Fully applies to my enterprise
Source: Own work

it means that half of Polish medium and large-sized enterprises do not employ any staff specialising in risk management. This may have a negative impact on the effectiveness of risk mitigation.

Almost 55% of the surveyed companies do not have a specialised organisational department that would holistically deal with risk management in the enterprise, and only 9.70% confirm that such a department is included in their organisational structure. Therefore, the risk management process is not formalised and systematic. This confirms the research carried out so far in the Polish economic reality, which shows that risk management departments are only created in very large-sized enterprises, mainly in listed enterprises.

The state of employee participation in risk management in the enterprise is slightly better. Only less than 25% of the surveyed enterprises claim that they do not involve employees in risk mitigation at all or their participation in this process is small. In turn, more than half of the surveyed medium and large-sized enterprises believe that employee participation applies to their enterprise at least partially. These results mean that most of the surveyed enterprises see the usefulness of employees in mitigating risk and know the benefits of both broader threats identification and assessment and more cautious employee behaviour. Theoretical considerations and research conducted so far show that the participation of employees in risk management may contribute to the improvement of the effectiveness of this process, and thus to reducing damage and losses.

The last two questions in the resource part of the survey related to the enterprise risk management system (RES4 and RES5 factors) and made it possible to identify the degree of advancement of the approach to risk mitigation and to identify the creators of the risk management systems used in the surveyed enterprises. The responses show that if an enterprise uses a systemic approach to risk mitigation, it is designed and implemented on its own without the participation of external entities. On the one hand, this allows to reduce the expenditure and costs, and on the other hand, it allows for a good adjustment of the developed methods and tools to the specificity and needs of the enterprise. However, it may be at risk of design or methodological errors, all the more so, as the results described above show, most of the surveyed enterprises do not employ experts in the field of risk management and do not have organisational departments dealing with risk mitigation in their organisation.

Only about 13% of the surveyed enterprises have advanced risk management systems. The assessment of this statement by the respondents is characterised by the lowest arithmetic mean, the mode and the value of the upper quartile, which means that such solutions are very rarely used in Polish enterprises. This is partly due to the fact that these are solutions dedicated to large enterprises, and partly because they require professional staff and appropriate organisational resources (Cheba & Saniuk, 2016). The surveyed enterprises cannot cope with the fulfilment of the latter two requirements, so likewise they are not interested in implementing advanced risk management systems known as Enterprise Risk Management (ERM).

In light of the responses to the methodological and resource factors, it can be stated that the surveyed enterprises mostly know and apply the basic principles of risk management. However, they do not use specialised solutions and tools. They mainly use their own managers and their own organisational resources to mitigate risks. They do not use external experts, nor do they order complex risk management systems. The main advantage of this approach to risk management is savings in financial resources, while the main disadvantage may be excessive self-confidence, resulting in errors in the risk management process.

The last group of determinants of the effectiveness of risk management are factors related to the sources of risk located in the internal and external environment. The assessment results of the statements concerning these factors are presented in Tables 6.7 and 6.8.

The first four questions in the section on the last group of risk management effectiveness determinants related to the internal determinants of economic risk. The first was of a general nature, making it possible to assess the perception of internal threats. Thus, only about 15% of the surveyed enterprises believe that the risk arising inside the enterprise poses a serious threat to its functioning. Most of the surveyed entities assume that such risk only affects them partially or not at all. This allows to confirm the conclusions included in the review part of this monograph, according to which the current key source of risk in enterprises is the external environment characterised by high variability, dynamism and amplitude of the observed changes. The real expression of these features is the progressive digitisation (Gajdzik & Wolniak, 2021; Saniuk &

Table 6.7 Responses for environmental factors (ENV)

Series	Descriptive variable	1	2	3	4	5
ENV1	The most serious threats arise inside the enterprise.	134 18.56%	227 31.44%	251 34.76%	85 11.77%	25 3.46%
ENV2	The most serious internal source of risk is human resources.	56 7.76%	138 19.11%	238 32.96%	198 27.42%	92 12.74%
ENV3	The most serious internal source of risk is the lack of financial liquidity.	261 36.15%	174 24.10%	124 17.17%	102 14.13%	61 8.45%
ENV4	The most serious internal source of risk is the lack of funds.	281 38.92%	156 21.61%	127 17.59%	89 12.33%	69 9.56%
ENV5	The relationships with suppliers are the most intense source of risk in an enterprise.	135 18.70%	225 31.16%	234 32.41%	101 13.99%	27 3.74%
ENV6	Relations with recipients are the most intense source of risk in an enterprise.	82	178	205	185	72
ENV7	The greatest source of risk is the enterprise's competition.	11.36% 117	24.65% 153	28.39% 210	25.62% 172	9.97% 70
ENV8	The enterprise is very sensitive to economic fluctuations.	16.20% 109 15.10%	21.19% 189 26.18%	29.09% 234 32.41%	23.82% 138 19.11%	9.70% 52 7.20%
ENV9	Changes in the international environment have a strong impact on the enterprise's operations.	200 27.70%	185 25.62%	176 24.38%	121 16.76%	40 5.54%

Assessment scale: (1) Does not apply to my enterprise. (2) Applies to my enterprise to a small extent. (3) Partially applies to my enterprise. (4) Applies to my enterprise to a significant extent. (5) Fully applies to my enterprise

Source: Own work

Saniuk, 2018; Zawiła-Niedźwiecki & Byczkowski, 2009) and the globalisation of economies and internationalisation of enterprises (Saniuk & Saniuk, 2017), but also the growing climate crisis and the Covid-19 pandemic. All these phenomena are characterised by unpredictability and the growing range of damages and threats related to their occurrence. In

Table 6.8 Responses for the risk exposure that related to the internal, proximal and distal environment (ENV)

Series	Average	Median	Mode	Mode size	Lower quartile	Upper quartile	Standard deviation	Coefficient of variation	Skewness	Kurtosis
ENV1	2.50	2.00	3.00	251.00	2.00	3.00	1.03	41.27	0.28	-0.41
ENV2	3.18	3.00	3.00	238.00	2.00	4.00	1.12	35.18	-0.15	-0.67
ENV3	2.35	2.00	1.00	261.00	1.00	3.00	1.32	56.24	0.60	-0.86
ENV4	2.32	2.00	1.00	281.00	1.00	3.00	1.35	58.13	0.65	-0.83
ENV5	2.53	3.00	3.00	234.00	2.00	3.00	1.06	42.01	0.28	-0.55
ENV6	2.98	3.00	3.00	205.00	2.00	4.00	1.17	39.07	-0.02	-0.87
ENV7	2.90	3.00	3.00	210.00	2.00	4.00	1.22	41.97	-0.02	-0.94
ENV8	2.77	3.00	3.00	234.00	2.00	4.00	1.14	41.05	0.13	-0.73
ENV9	2.47	2.00	1.00	200.00	2.00	3.00	1.03	41.27	0.28	-0.41

Key:
ENV1: The most serious threats arise inside the enterprise
ENV2: The most serious internal source of risk is human resources
ENV3: The most serious internal source of risk is the lack of financial liquidity
ENV4: The most serious internal source of risk is the lack of funds
ENV5: The relationships with suppliers are the most intense source of risk in an enterprise
ENV6: Relations with recipients are the most intense source of risk in an enterprise
ENV7: The greatest source of risk is the enterprise's competition
ENV8: The enterprise is very sensitive to economic fluctuations
ENV9: Changes in the international environment have a strong impact on the enterprise's operations
Assessment scale: (1) Does not apply to my enterprise. (2) Applies to my enterprise to a small extent. (3) Partially applies to my enterprise. (4) Applies to my enterprise to a significant extent. (5) Fully applies to my enterprise
Source: Own work

addition, their impact on the activities of enterprises increases interpenetration and accumulation of risk sources.

More detailed questions concerning internal threats allowed to create their general hierarchy. The results of this ranking are presented in Fig. 6.2.

The data presented in Fig. 6.2 shows that the surveyed enterprises primarily associate internal threats with human resources. This means that mistakes, errors and negligence of employees are the most intense source of threats for enterprises, despite the control that owners and managers have over those they employ. However, this control cannot be exercised without end. Moreover, human nature is unpredictable. It is also worth adding that any accidents or irregularities in the workplace are borne by the employer, i.e. the surveyed enterprises. The effects associated with their occurrence may entail additional financial and even criminal burdens, hence the fear of such threats by enterprises is quite significant. Endangering human health and life is also an additional mental burden, which does not occur to such a great extent when material resources are exposed to risk.

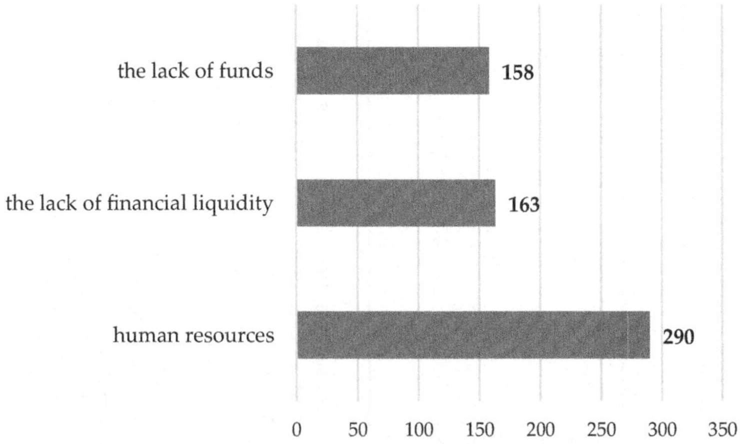

Fig. 6.2 Assessment of the intensity of internal threats (percentage of indications: (4) Applies to my enterprise to a significant extent. (5) Fully applies to my enterprise). (Source: Own work)

The surveyed enterprises are much less afraid of the lack of financial resources and the loss of financial liquidity, despite the fact that the latter is the most common cause of enterprise bankruptcy. This may be due to the lack of a sense of the current threat in such situations or the confidence of the management as to whether they are able to cope with these circumstances. A very low fear of the indicated sources of risk may also be the result of the long market experience of the surveyed enterprises and good economic conditions in the period in which the study was conducted. Nevertheless, it is worth adding that while enterprises agree on the issue of perceiving human resources as a source of risk (as proved by the relatively low value of the coefficient of variation and the range between the upper and lower quartile), in the case of a lack of liquidity or financial resources, the differentiation of opinions is significantly higher (this is confirmed by the high coefficient of variation and the greater range between the upper and lower quartile). Thus, financial risks are perceived by managers in quite different ways, which may be influenced by, among other things, a different history of experiences, and thus the perception of risk too.

The next three survey questions referred to the sources of risk related to the proximal environment. Accordingly, they concerned relations with: suppliers, recipients and competition of the surveyed enterprises. The assessment of the intensity of these threats is presented synthetically in Fig. 6.3.

Thus, for the surveyed enterprises, the most intense source of risk is relationships with recipients. Over 35% of respondents believe that this threat largely or fully affects their enterprise. This means that Polish enterprises most often and most strongly fear losing the sales market, and thus the possibility of generating income and financial profits. For a slightly smaller group (approx. 33%), an important source of risk is also competition, which may take over existing and future customers. The responses also show that the surveyed enterprises are much less afraid of disruptions in relations with suppliers. Only about 17% of managers assign this factor an assessment of 4 and 5. This means that the surveyed enterprises can quite freely choose and decide on the sources of supply, and thus effectively mitigate the risk related to the continuity and sufficiency of production/service provision. It is also worth adding that in

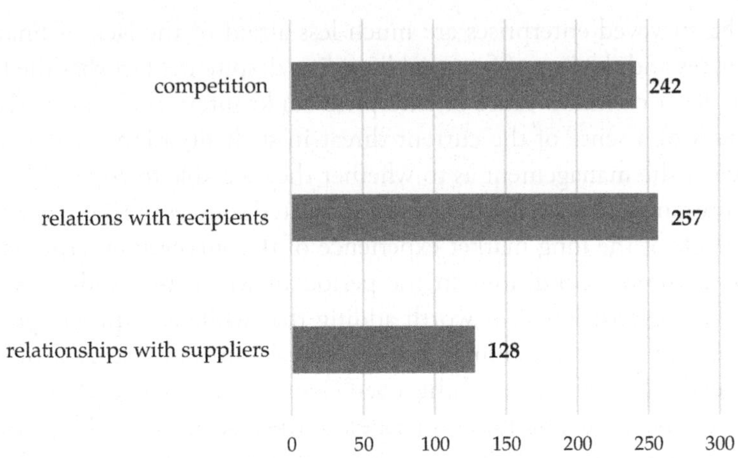

Fig. 6.3 Assessment of the intensity of threats related to the proximal environment: recipients, suppliers and competition (percentage of indications: (4) Applies to my enterprise to a significant extent. (5) Fully applies to my enterprise). (Source: Own work)

their assessments of the proximal environment as a source of risk, responders are quite consistent, as proved by the average values of the coefficients of variation and low values of the skewness of the distribution of responses.

The last two statements included in the section identifying the intensity of risk sources related to the environment of the surveyed enterprises concerned the distal environment. In the national context, this environment represented the question of economic volatility. The global context was reflected in the question of changes in the international environment. The distribution of the highest assessments (4 and 5) of the respondents for both questions is shown in Fig. 6.4.

According to the data presented in Fig. 6.4, fluctuations in the economic situation are considered by the respondents as a greater threat to the conducted activity than changes on the international market. Nevertheless, this is not a big difference, which means that about a quarter of managers of Polish medium and large-sized enterprises are afraid of changes in the distal environment, which may have a significant impact on their financial results and value. It should also be added that the

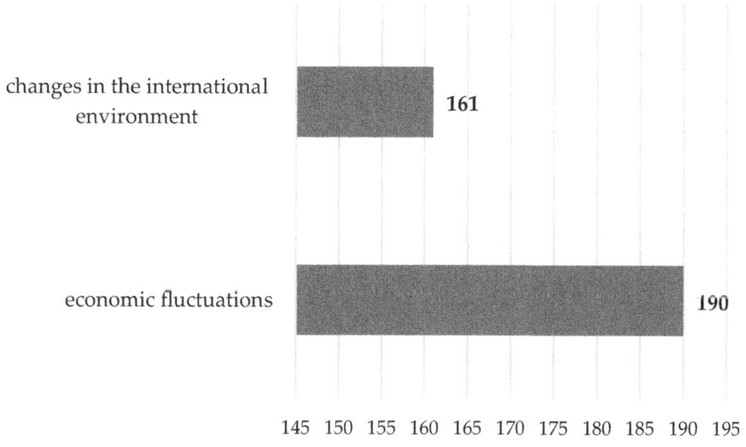

Fig. 6.4 Assessment of the intensity of threats related to the distal environment: economic situation and changes in the international environment (percentage of indications: (4) Applies to my enterprise to a significant extent. (5) Fully applies to my enterprise). (Source: Own work)

average values of the coefficient of variation and skewness of the distribution prove the like-mindedness of the respondents with regard to the perception and assessment of the intensity of risk sources in the distal environment of the enterprise.

In this context, it is worth explaining that the Polish enterprises are poorly internationalised, and therefore direct exposure to risk may apply to them to a limited extent from the outset. Nevertheless, they see threats of the systematic internationalisation of national economies, which may then also affect them, even if it is only an indirect impact.

As part of the summary of the environmental determinants of the effectiveness of risk management, Fig. 6.5 presents the value of the average assessments given by the surveyed enterprises for individual threats related to the interior, proximal and distal environment.

According to the data presented in Fig. 6.5, despite declarations of a relatively low fear of internal threats, the surveyed enterprises consider human resources to be the most intense source of risk. The proximal environment, including in particular relations with customers and competition, also generates a great risk for them. In turn, Polish small and

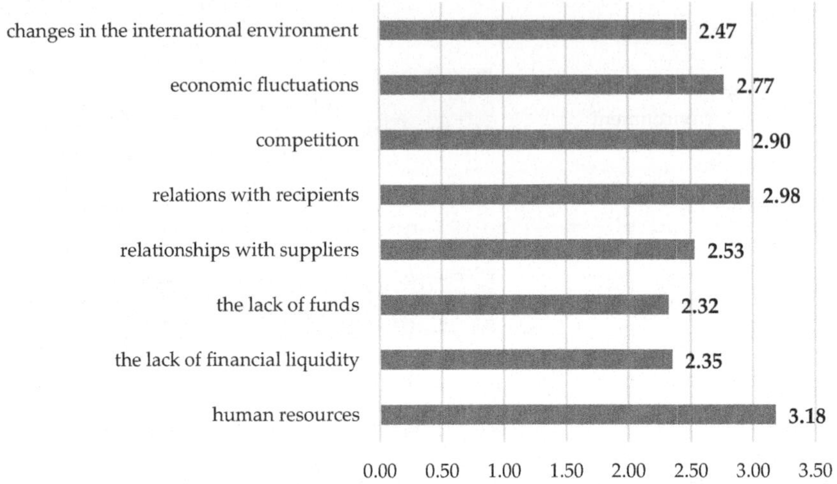

Fig. 6.5 Average assessments given by the surveyed enterprises for individual threats related to the interior, proximal and distal environment. (Source: Own work)

medium-sized enterprises assess the lowest risk related to the lack of liquidity, lack of financial resources and changes in the international environment. Such results show that the closer a given source of potential threats is to the enterprise, the greater it causes concern and uncertainty. As the distance increases, i.e. moving from the interior and the proximal environment to the international and distal environment, the assessment of threats systematically decreases. Managers therefore believe that internal and competitive conditions have the greatest impact on their performance, and therefore also the level of risk.

Apart from the determinants of the effectiveness of risk management, the questionnaire also included questions relating to the scope of effectiveness itself in three perspectives (Zawiła-Niedźwiecki, 2010, 2012):

1. referring to the implementation of the basic objectives of risk management, i.e. risk and loss prevention;
2. relating to the enterprise's short term goal of survival on the market;
3. referring to the long term goal of the enterprise's operation, which is to build value for all stakeholders associated with the enterprise's development.

The list of assessments of the surveyed enterprises is presented in Tables 6.9 and 6.10. Additionally—to better illustrate the results of the effectiveness assessment—the sum of the number of the highest assessments (4 and 5) is shown in Fig. 6.6.

In light of the obtained results, it can be stated that almost half of the surveyed enterprises positively assess the effectiveness of risk management in all three perspectives. This means a rational and positive attitude to the methods and tools for mitigating risks and is a very good proof of the competences of the management of the surveyed enterprises.

The relatively high values of the lower quartile, amounting to 3.00, for statements concerning the minimisation of damage and threats and development support also prove a positive assessment of the effectiveness of risk management. This means that only 25% of the surveyed enterprises have a bad or very bad assessment of the effects of using risk management methods and tools in the enterprise.

Interestingly, the effectiveness of risk management is best assessed in the long term as a factor supporting enterprise development. Companies are less likely to see risk management as just a means of survival. The difference is not significant, but it shows that risk management is associated with very positive effects for business.

Table 6.9 Responses to effectiveness of risk management (EF)

Series	Descriptive variable	1	2	3	4	5
EF1	Risk management in the enterprise minimises risks and losses.	63 8.73%	96 13.30%	203 28.12%	227 31.44%	133 18.42%
EF2	Risk management in the enterprise enables survival in the market.	85 11.77%	115 15.93%	182 25.21%	218 30.19%	122 16.90%
EF3	Risk management supports the development of the enterprise.	69 9.56%	103 14.27%	186 25.76%	232 32.13%	132 18.28%

Assessment scale: (1) Does not apply to my enterprise. (2) Applies to my enterprise to a small extent. (3) Partially applies to my enterprise. (4) Applies to my enterprise to a significant extent. (5) Fully applies to my enterprise

Source: Own work

Table 6.10 Responses to assessing the effectiveness of risk management (EF)

Series	Average	Median	Mode	Mode size	Lower quartile	Upper quartile	Standard deviation	Coefficient of variation	Skewness	Kurtosis
EF1	3.38	3.00	4.00	227.00	3.00	4.00	1.18	34.98	-0.40	-0.63
EF2	3.25	3.00	4.00	218.00	2.00	4.00	1.25	38.37	-0.31	-0.88
EF3	3.35	4.00	4.00	232.00	3.00	4.00	1.21	35.97	-0.40	-0.72

Key:
EF1: Risk management in the enterprise minimises risks and losses
EF2: Risk management in the enterprise enables survival in the market
EF3: Risk management supports the development of the enterprise
Assessment scale: (1) Does not apply to my enterprise. (2) Applies to my enterprise to a small extent. (3) Partially applies to my enterprise. (4) Applies to my enterprise to a significant extent. (5) Fully applies to my enterprise
Source: Own work

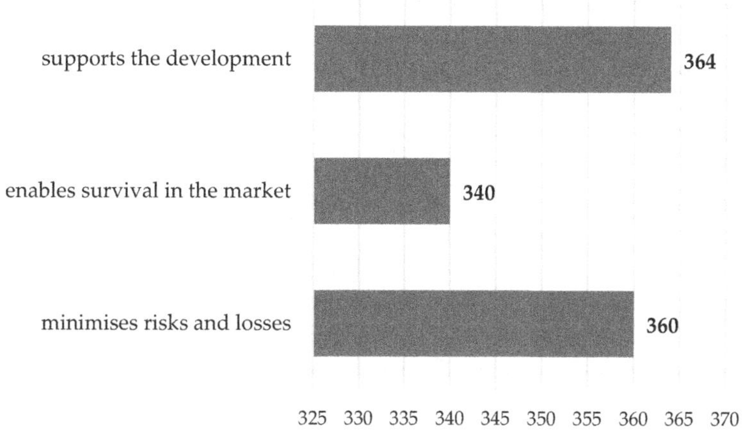

Fig. 6.6 Assessment of the effectiveness of risk management—sum of numbers for the highest assessment values ((4) Applies to my enterprise to a significant extent. (5) Fully applies to my enterprise). (Source: Own work)

It is also worth adding that those enterprises very positively assessing the effectiveness of risk management are quite consistent in their opinions, which is reflected in the average and similar values of the coefficient of variation.

References

Cheba, K., & Saniuk, S. (2016). Wielowymiarowa analiza wykorzystania technologii ICT w przedsiębiorstwach w Polsce. *Przedsiębiorczość i Zarządzanie, 17*(12), 41–53.

Gajdzik, B., & Wolniak, R. (2021). Digitalisation and innovation in the steel industry in Poland—Selected tools of ICT in an analysis of statistical data and a case study. *Energies, 14*(11), 3034.

Jonek-Kowalska, I. (2020a). Behawioralne aspekty zarządzania ryzykiem w polskich przedsiębiorstwach w świetle badań ankietowych. [W:] E. Sońta-Drączkowska & I. Bednarska-Wnuk (Red.), *Wybrane aspekty zarządzania procesami, projektami i ryzykiem w przedsiębiorstwach* (pp. 231–244). Wydawnictwo Uniwersytetu Łódzkiego.

Jonek-Kowalska, I. (2020b). Ocena stopnia zaawansowania zarządzania ryzykiem z perspektywy rodzaju prowadzonej działalności gospodarczej w polskich przedsiębiorstwach. [W:]. D. Kopycińska & J. Korpysa (Eds.), *Współczesne problemy gospodarowania* (pp. 207–220). Fundacja Centrum Badań Socjologicznych.

Saniuk, S., & Saniuk, A. (2017). Analiza sytuacji polskich przedsiębiorstw w sieciach przemysłowych w dobie Industry 4.0. *Nauki o Zarządzaniu. Uniwersytet Ekonomiczny we Wrocławiu, 2*(31), 12–17.

Saniuk, S., & Saniuk, A. (2018). Challenges of industry 4.0 for production enterprises functioning within cyber industry networks. *Management Systems in Production Engineering, 4*(26), 212–216.

Zawiła-Niedźwiecki, J. (2010). Pojęcie ryzyka operacyjnego i klasyfikacja jego rodzajów. *Przegląd Organizacji, 6*, 19–21.

Zawiła-Niedźwiecki, J. (2012). Analiza ryzyka operacyjnego z perspektywy teorii organizacji. *Zeszyty Naukowe Uniwersytetu Szczecińskiego. Finanse, Rynki Finansowe, Ubezpieczenia, 51*, 179–189.

Zawiła-Niedźwiecki, J., & Byczkowski, M. (2009). Information security aspect of operational risk management. *Foundations of Management, 1*(2), 45–64.

7

Practical Dimension of Risk Management Effectiveness: Results of Research in Polish Enterprises

7.1 Methodological Assumptions

In the course of research on the relationships between particular groups of determinants and the effectiveness of risk management in the enterprise, structural equation modeling was used (Hershberger, 2003; Cliff, 1983). This method allows for the analysis of complex relationships between many variables and therefore it can be used in the research model proposed in the paper.

In practice, it is very often used in the field of economics, social sciences and humanities, because it allows to systematise the results of multi-faceted questionnaire research containing behavioural observations and subjective opinions of respondents (Staniec, 2012). This is done thanks to the possibility of parameterising unobservable and non-quantifiable factors in the form of certain latent variables, then aggregated to specific groups of endogenous variables ultimately affecting the examined exogenous variable.

An additional advantage of modeling structural equations is the possibility of taking into account indirect relationships between individual groups of variables, which is not possible with classical multiple

I. Jonek-Kowalska, *Effectiveness of Enterprise Risk Management*,
https://doi.org/10.1007/978-3-030-95376-8_7

regression, most often used in the process of identifying the dependencies and effects of independent variables on the dependent variable.

Structural equation modeling takes place in three stages including (Zasuwa, 2011; Baumgartner & Homburg, 1996):

1. theoretical definition of the model,
2. model identification,
3. estimating model parameters,
4. determining the goodness of fit of the model,
5. modification of the model.

The first of these stages is considered to be the most important. Its task is to determine the basic relationships between the analysed variables. These relationships are identified and described on the basis of the existing economic, social and humanistic regularities reflected and confirmed in previous scientific research (MacKenzie & Lutz, 1989). Therefore, the development of the model requires thorough literature studies, experience and knowledge of the phenomena studied. Without it, a valid structural equation model cannot be developed. The next steps are only computational processes aimed at determining the strength and direction of the researched relations and their credibility.

And so, it is possible to parameterise it at the level of model identification. The necessary condition in this case is the fulfilment of the *t* rule, according to which the number of estimated parameters should be less than or equal to the number of unique values in the covariance matrix. In turn, the number of unique values can be calculated using the formula 7.1:

$$u = p \times (p+1)/2 \tag{7.1}$$

where:*p*—number of observed variables.

Fulfilment of the above mentioned relationship is a guarantee of the model's traceability. In practice, helping to possibly meet it are the following guidelines (Schumacker & Lomax, 2004):

- In the model, one factor load should be set as 1 for each unobservable variable or the variance of latent variables at the unity level should be specified.
- Models with feedback relationships between variables, that is the non-recursive models, should be avoided.
- Only the most important variables should be entered into the model and the same approach should be used for defining the relationship between the selected variables.

After finding the possibility of identifying the model, you can start estimating the parameters of the model, i.e. determining the strength and direction of the relationships linking the individual variables selected and characterised in the first stage. From a statistical point of view, estimating the model consists in finding such values of individual model parameters that will enable the most faithful replication of the observed real covariance matrix (Kacprzak, 2018; Konarski, 2009).

Four methods that can be used in the process of model estimation are described below (Zasuwa, 2011):

1. *ML—maximum likelihood*: requires meeting the assumption of multidimensional normality of an observable variable; applicable with fewer attempts; resistant to change of the measuring scale; it cannot be used when the observed covariance matrix is not positively determined;
2. *GLS—generalised least squares*: requires meeting the assumption of multivariate normality of an observable variable; applicable with fewer attempts; can be used when the observed covariance matrix is not positively determined;
3. *USL—unweighted least squares*: may not require meeting the assumption of multivariate normality of an observable variable (however, then it is not possible to estimate the model measurement errors); applicable with fewer attempts; can be used when the observed covariance matrix is not positively determined;
4. *WLS—weighted least squares = ADF—asymptotically distribution free*: does not require meeting the assumption of multidimensional normality of an observable variable; can be used with very numerous trials, at least 200–500 observations;

Model testing, which is the penultimate stage of creating structural equations, means the assessment of the fit of real data to the model form, i.e. checking to what extent the obtained model allows to replicate the input covariance matrix. Typically, the following indicators are used in the testing process (Kline, 2005):

- *GFI—goodness-of-fit index*: allows to determine what part of the variance in the observed matrix is explained by the identified model of structural equations; the satisfactory value of this indicator is 0.95 and more;
- *AGFI—adjusted goodness-of-fit index*: this is the degrees of freedom adjusted version of the GFI indicator;
- *RMSEA—root mean square error of approximation*: this is the value of the root mean square error of approximation; 0.05 or less is considered a satisfactory value.

The estimation of the model parameters may turn out to be unsatisfactory due to the failure to achieve the satisfactory values of the indicators indicated above. Then an attempt should be made to modify the model aimed at improving the fit. Most often, statistically insignificant relationships are removed from the model. You can also change the relationships between selected groups of variables and / or introduce new, justified relationships between the variables. However, it is worth emphasising that the search for a perfect fit model should not be an end in itself. It may turn out that the studied entities or phenomena do not reflect the required economic or social regularities, and the search for an ideal model leads to a distortion of recommendations or theoretical rules (Richter et al., 2016).

In the case of assessing the effectiveness of risk management in an enterprise, as presented in this monograph, the original model of structural equations was determined on the basis of the literature studies shown in the initial theoretical chapters. Its character is presented in the methodological chapter summarising literature studies and constituting an introduction to the research part. The next chapter presents the results of structural modeling obtained using the *Statistica* software in the SEPATH module.

7.2 Assessment of the Determinants of Risk Management Effectiveness

Latent variables used in the process of structural modeling meet the requirements of normal distribution, with a few exceptions, because the kurtosis and skewness coefficient do not exceed the value of 1 (see Chap. 6). And in the case of a little observed exceedance, their value is insignificant (kurtosis much lower than 7—limit value of moderate deviations from the normal distribution) (Curran et al., 1996). The identified regularities made it possible to use the estimation model defined in the *Statistica* package as GLS → ML for structural modeling.

In the first stage of the research, the parameters of the initial model, developed on the basis of the aforementioned literature studies, were estimated. Its assumptions are presented in Chap. 5 of this monograph in detail. The estimation results for individual model paths are presented in Table 7.1 and Fig. 7.1.

Table 7.1 Parameters of the structural model in the base version compliant with the theoretical assumptions

Path	Coefficient	*T*-Statistics	Probability
Correlation paths of endogenous variables			
behavioural factors (BEH) → resources involved in risk management (RES)	-0.274	-6.382	0.000
behavioural factors (BEH) → methodology of risk management (RM)	0.382	9.673	0.000
environmental factors (ENV) → resources involved in risk management (RES)	0.045	1.115	0.265
environmental factors (ENV) → methodology of risk management (RM)	-0.182	-4.821	0.000
Paths of influence of endogenous variables on an exogenous variable			
behavioural factors (BEH) → effectiveness of risk management (EF)	0.070	0.966	0.334
methodology of risk management (RM) → effectiveness of risk management (EF)	1.072	13.439	0.000
resources involved in risk management (RES) → effectiveness of risk management (EF)	0.456	7.177	0.000
environmental factors (ENV) → effectiveness of risk management (EF)	0.024	0.440	0.660
Goodness of fit assessment	$\chi^2(426) = 3292.71$ $p = 0.000$ GFI = 0.748 AGFI = 0.707 RMSEA = 0.102		

Source: Own work

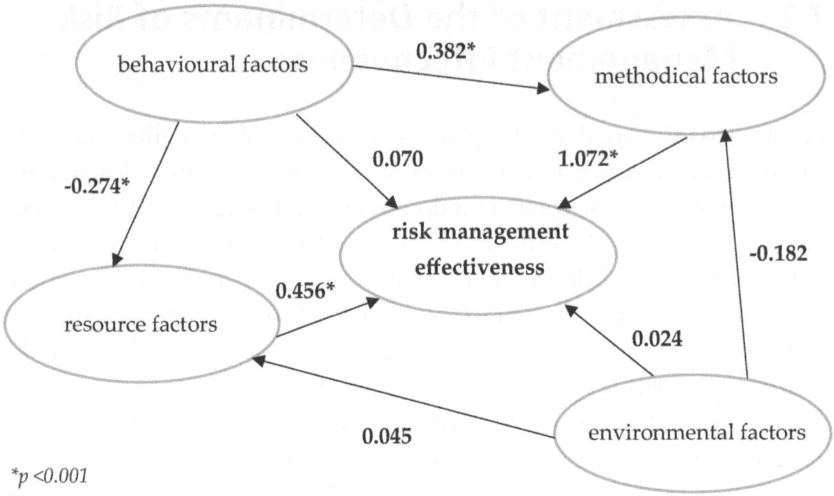

Fig. 7.1 Structural parameters in model 1 (base version). (Source: Own work, *$p < 0.001$)

In the estimated model, four out of eight path coefficients are statistically significant, which allows to confirm the following relationships between the determinants of risk management effectiveness:

- the impact of behavioural factors on the resources involved in risk management,
- the impact of behavioural factors on the methodology of risk management in the enterprise,
- the impact of environmental factors on the methodology of risk management in the enterprise,

and the impact of the following determinants on risk management effectiveness (exogenous model variable):

- risk management methodology,
- resources involved in risk management.

Nevertheless, it is worth noting that the goodness of fit indicators obtained for the analysed model are not satisfactory. The GFI index means that only 74.8% of the real variances is explained by the obtained model of structural equations. An even lower value of the fit is indicated by the AGFI adjusted to the number of degrees of freedom. RMSEA also exceeds the acceptable value. Therefore, as part of the research, the obtained model was modified many times by removing statistically insignificant relations and testing various combinations of relations between exogenous and endogenous variables, assuming their rationality, which is confirmed in previous research and literature on the subject. As a result, a model was obtained with a better, though not fully satisfactory, goodness fit. The results of the estimation of this model are shown in Fig. 7.2 and Table 7.2.

In such a parameterised model, all path coefficients are statistically significant, and the goodness of fit is described by higher GFI and AGFI values and a lower RMSEA value than in the original theoretical model. The resulting modified model shows the relationship between:

- behavioural factors and risk management methodology,
- and the resources involved in risk management and the risk management methodology.

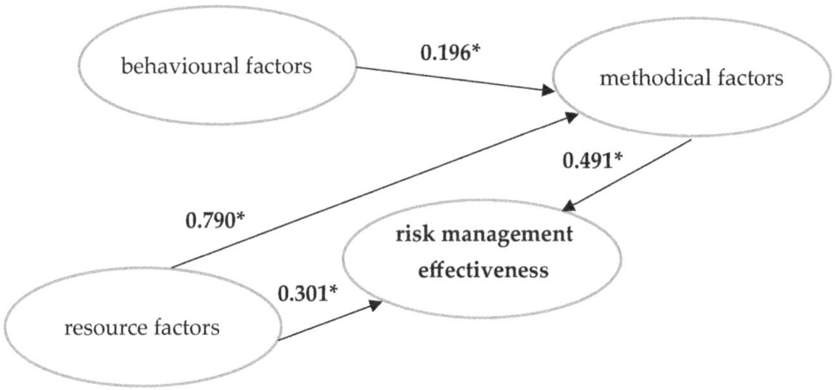

*p <0.001

Fig. 7.2 Structural parameters in model 2 (corrected—after removing statistically insignificant paths). (Source: Own work, $*p < 0.001$)

Table 7.2 Parameters of the structural model in the corrected version with a better model fit

Path	Coefficient	*T*-Statistics	Probability
Correlation paths of endogenous variables			
behavioural factors (BEH) → methodology of risk management (RM)	0.196	5.861	0.000
resources involved in risk management (RES) → methodology of risk management (RM)	0.790	37.981	0.000
Paths of influence of endogenous variables on an exogenous variable			
methodology of risk management (RM) → effectiveness of risk management (EF)	0.491	8.280	0.000
resources involved in risk management (RES) → effectiveness of risk management (EF)	0.301	5.037	0.000
Goodness of fit assessment	χ^2 (430) = 2936.40 p = 0.000 GFI = 0.756 AGFI = 0.719 RMSEA = 0.098		

Source: Own work

In addition, it allows to conclude that risk management effectiveness is primarily influenced by:

- risk management methodology,
- and resources involved in risk management.

Therefore, both models show the significance of the impact of methodological and resource factors on risk management effectiveness. The impact of methodological factors is greater than that of resource factors. Therefore, it can be concluded that the more enterprises use advanced methods of risk management and the greater the scope of protection applied, the more effective risk management is. This means that the correct selection of risk management instruments and a wide range of protection guaranteed by them, as well as the competences and knowledge of human resources, are factors that allow enterprises to limit threats and losses in the short term and favour the development of enterprises in the long term.

Looking at the detailed description of the latent variables in the risk management methodology category, it can be concluded that the effectiveness of risk management is positively influenced by the completeness of the management process, including: identification, assessment, selection of risk management methods and risk control. When analysing the resource context, it can be concluded that the involvement of experts can also have a positive impact on the effectiveness of risk management. As does the use of more advanced risk management systems and the separation of a department in the organisational structure dealing with this process. Employee participation is also an important resource factor. Its increase may simulate an improvement in the effectiveness of risk management.

Both the original structural model and the modified model do not confirm the direct influence of behavioural and environmental factors on the effectiveness of risk management. In the case of environmental determinants, their indirect impact on the effectiveness of risk management in the enterprise was not found either. This means that these factors are treated by the surveyed managers as variables that they are not able to shape. They can only predict them at the stage of threats identyfication and assessment as part of the key steps in the risk and loss prevention process. Theoretically, such perception of environmental factors is rational due to the previously described lack of the enterprise's ability to influence the immediate and distant surroundings.

Nevertheless, the results obtained in this respect may also indicate that the surveyed Polish enterprises do not adapt the scope and methodology of risk management to changes observed in the environment, treating them as certain procedures permanently included in management and not requiring modification under the influence of external factors. Such observations may also result from the economic conditions in which the survey was conducted. This was the period before the Covid-19 pandemic, characterised by stable and sustained gross domestic product growth, low unemployment and inflation in Poland. Therefore, managers operated in fairly safe conditions, without a sense of increased threat, which in a way lulls the vigilance and sensitivity to changes and turbulence of the external environment. Unfortunately, it is also not a good prognosis in the context of protection against the consequences of such a crisis as brought about by the coronavirus pandemic, because it may suggest disregarding threats, partially confirmed in the analysis of behavioural factors too.

With regard to behavioural factors, in both models, no direct, statistically significant impact on the effectiveness of risk management in the enterprise was found. Nevertheless, both models confirm the indirect influence of these determinants on the prevention of threats and losses in the enterprise. Behavioural factors influence the methodology of risk management, which means that the perception of risk and attitudes towards risk determine decisions regarding the selection of tools limiting the scale of threats and losses in the enterprise. This means that the negative perception of risk and the often accompanying risk aversion induce enterprises to increase the level of protection against threats and losses. This attitude seems to be justified and rational. It also makes the enterprise safer, because the managers are aware of the existence of risk sources, and they are afraid of their occurrence and react preventively. Nevertheless, it is worth adding that in extreme cases, emphasised in the theoretical part, the excessive fear of risk and safeguarding in taking up challenges may become a factor inhibiting the development of entrepreneurship and innovation. In the current Polish economic conditions (Poland is on one of the last places in terms of the level of innovation in Europe), the dissemination of such attitudes would constitute an additional obstacle in the process of domestic economic development.

Summing up the results obtained in the course of structural modeling, the following statements should be considered the most important conclusions:

- The effectiveness of risk management in the surveyed Polish large and medium-sized enterprises is primarily determined by methodological factors related to the selection and scope of risk management methods.
- Additionally, it is influenced by the scope of human, organisational and financial resources involved in the risk management process in the enterprise.

- Neither behavioural factors related to the decision maker nor environmental factors related to the functioning of enterprises in the immediate and distant environment have a direct impact on the effectiveness of risk management.
- However, behavioural factors affect the methodology of risk management in the enterprise, which means that as the fear of threats and losses grows, the level and scope of protection against the occurrence of risk increases.
- Environmental factors cannot be shaped by enterprises and most likely for this reason they were not included in the models for assessing the effectiveness of risk management in the enterprise.

References

Baumgartner, H., & Homburg, C. (1996). Application of structural equation modelling in marketing and consumer research. A review. *International Journal of Research in Marketing, 13*, 139–161.

Cliff, N. (1983). Some cautions concerning the application of causal modeling methods. *Multivariate Behavioral Research, 18*, 115–126.

Curran, P. J., West, S. G., & Finch, J. F. (1996). The robustness of test statistic to nonnormality and specification error in confirmatory factor analysis. *Psychological Methods, 3*, 424–453.

Hershberger, S. L. (2003). The growth of structural equation modeling: 1994–2001 structural equation modeling. *A Multidisciplinary Journal, 10*(1), 35–46.

Kacprzak, A. (2018). Modelowanie strukturalne w analizie zachowań konsumentów: porównanie metod opartych na analizie kowariancji (CB-SEM) i częściowych najmniejszych kwadratów (PLS-SEM). *Handel Wewnętrzny, 6*(377), 247–261.

Kline, R. B. (2005). *Principles and practice of structural equation modeling.* The Guilford Press.

Konarski, R. (2009). *Modele równań strukturalnych. Teoria i praktyka.* Wydawnictwo Naukowe PWN.

MacKenzie, S. B., & Lutz, R. J. (1989). An empirical examination of the structural antecedents of attitude toward the ad in an advertising pretesting context. *Journal of Marketing, 53*, 48–65.

Richter, N. F., Sinkovics, R. R., Ringle, C. M., & Schlägel, C. (2016). A critical look at the use of SEM in international business research. *International Marketing Review, 33*(3), 67–81.

Schumacker, R. M., & Lomax, R. G. (2004). *A beginner's guide to structural equation modeling*. Lawrence Erlbaum Associates Publishers.

Staniec, I. (2012). Modelowanie równań strukturalnych w naukach o zarządzaniu. *Organizacja i Kierowanie, 2*, 65–88.

Zasuwa, G. (2011). *Zastosowanie modelowania równań strukturalnych do badań nad zachowaniem konsumentów*. StatSoft Polska. DaneWiedzaSukces.pl.

8

How to Improve Risk Management Effectiveness?: Conclusions and Recommendations

8.1 Conclusions from Research on Risk Management Effectiveness

This chapter focuses on the main conclusions of the considerations and research carried out. Their formulation will become the starting point for the second subchapter containing recommendations for improving risk management effectiveness in the enterprise.

And so, theoretical considerations show that risk management is a systematic process that includes four basic stages: identification, assessment, selection and use of methods and tools securing the enterprise against risk, and risk control (Brustbauer, 2016). These stages must occur sequentially, and errors and shortcomings in their implementation carry over from stage to stage and result in a reduction in the effectiveness of risk management. In this monograph, this effectiveness is understood as the degree of protection of the enterprise against internal and external threats, obtained as a result of actions taken as part of risk management. Its assessment and monitoring are important because the financial results and efficiency of the entire enterprise directly depend on it. In extreme cases, the

I. Jonek-Kowalska, *Effectiveness of Enterprise Risk Management*,
https://doi.org/10.1007/978-3-030-95376-8_8

lack of effective protection against risk may lead to the bankruptcy of the enterprise or even the entire industry.

Separation of the determinants of the effectiveness of risk management in the enterprise was carried out on the basis of literature studies in the field of risk management. In this way, four groups of factors (conditions) were created that can potentially affect the degree to which the enterprise is secured against risk. These factors are:

1. behavioural—related to the perception and attitudes of managers towards risk;
2. methodological, relating to the completeness of the risk management process and instruments used in the course of risk mitigation;
3. resource—taking into account the type and scope of human, organisational and financial resources involved in the risk management process in the enterprise;
4. environmental—related to the intensity and frequency of occurrence of risk sources in the immediate and distant environment of the enterprise

Research on the impact of the aforementioned conditions on the effectiveness of risk management in an enterprise was carried out on a representative group of 722 Polish large and medium-sized enterprises. The obtained results were analysed in two stages. The first one included a general analysis of the respondents' replies to the survey questions and their assessment using descriptive statistics. The most important conclusions in this regard, with reference to the aforementioned groups of determinants, are presented in Table 8.1.

The results obtained in relation to behavioural factors confirm the previous conclusions regarding managers and entrepreneurs, according to which they are people with an above average tendency to take risks, willing to take up challenges and being a driving force of entrepreneurship and innovation (Cui et al., 2016; Wang et al., 2016). Nevertheless, in the case of Polish large and medium-sized enterprises, these are not decision makers willing to take significant risks, even if they do come with above average, potential benefits. This may be due to the relatively short period of functioning of the Polish economy in free market conditions and the

Table 8.1 Conclusions from the general analysis of risk management determinants in Polish large and medium-sized enterprises

Group of determinants	Conclusions
Behavioural	Most polish managers not only perceive risk in the category of a threat but also an opportunity. Polish managers like risk and are not afraid to take it, which corresponds and most likely results from a positive perception of this phenomenon. Despite a positive perception of risk and a high propensity to risk, polish enterprises do not want to engage in risky ventures. External threats are of much greater concern among the surveyed enterprises than internal threads, treated as manageable and controllable.
Methodical	The vast majority of the studied enterprises declare an active attitude towards risk aimed at limiting the risks and their possible consequences. The vast majority of the surveyed enterprises identify and describe the sources of risk, however, a quarter of polish medium and large-sized enterprises do not know what threats they may encounter and what losses they may cause in the course of their operations. Among the methods of risk management, the surveyed enterprises most often use economic insurance as a financial method of risk mitigation. Prevention as a typical form of material risk control is slightly less popular. A significant part of the respondents also use other forms of risk transfer for a fee (e.g. derivatives) and establish economic cooperation with other market entities in order to mitigate threats. The main reason for the lack of security against risk in the minority group of enterprises described above is the lack or insufficient level of financial resources. Most of the surveyed enterprises also carry out a risk management audit, which is the last step in this process. The group of about 15–20% of enterprises that do not take measures to reduce, identify or assess risk and do not undertake efforts to mitigate it should be assessed negatively.

(*continued*)

Table 8.1 (continued)

Group of determinants	Conclusions
Resource	Resource factors are assessed the worst among the analysed determinants. Only about 1/5 of the surveyed medium and large-sized enterprises employ experts in the field of risk management. More than half of the surveyed companies do not have a specialised organizational department that would holistically deal with risk management in the enterprise. About ¾ of the surveyed enterprises try to involve their employees in the risk management process. If the surveyed enterprises apply a systemic approach to risk mitigation, it is designed and implemented on their own without the participation of external entities. Only about 13% of the surveyed enterprises have advanced risk management systems.
Environmental	Only about 15% of the surveyed enterprises believe that the risk arising inside the enterprise poses a serious threat to its functioning. The surveyed enterprises primarily associate internal threats with human resources. The surveyed enterprises are much less afraid of the lack of financial resources and the loss of financial liquidity, despite the fact that the latter is the most common cause of enterprise bankruptcy. For the surveyed enterprises, the most intense source of external risk are relationships with customers. For about 1/3 of the respondents, a significant source of risk is also competition, which may take over existing and future customers. Fluctuations in the economic situation are considered by the respondents as a greater threat to the conducted activity than changes on the international market.

Source: Own work

traditional structure of industry, dominated by traditional industries with a low or average level of innovation. The indicated circumstances do not encourage and do not directly motivate to take risky and pro-innovative activities.

The responses of Polish large and medium-sized enterprises also confirm that the greatest source of risk in their operations is the contemporary, exceptionally turbulent economic surroundings, which they fear much more than internal problems and irregularities (Sengupta & Fanchon, 2009; Hoogvelt et al., 1987). It is worth adding that the identified concerns were even valid in the situation of a fairly stable economic situation in Poland before the Covid-19 pandemic, when the aforementioned survey was carried out. Therefore, it can be assumed that the pandemic has significantly increased the fear of enterprises of external threats. It is also natural that it multiplied the possible amplitude and frequency of changes in the economic conditions in which modern enterprises operate (Mishra, 2020).

When assessing the conditions relating to the risk management methodology in Polish large and medium-sized enterprises it can be concluded on the basis of submitted declarations that approximately 80% of the surveyed entities know the essence, purpose and course of the risk management process. These enterprises identify and assess threats. They choose methods and techniques for risk mitigation. Finally, they monitor and control the effects of risk management. Nevertheless, they use very traditional instruments in the form of business insurance and prevention in risk management. Such an approach may not be sufficient, especially in the context of the current economic downturn and the possibility of its deepening and rapid spread on an international scale.

The fact that Polish large and medium-sized enterprises are insufficiently prepared for external threats is also confirmed by the low involvement of human, organisational and financial resources in the risk management process. This suggests relying only on one's own knowledge and experience in risk mitigation, which is always subject to subjectivism and may lead to excessive self-confidence, thus underestimating both the threats themselves and the need to take actions to limit the effects of their occurrence. Meanwhile, even in the conditions of limited financial resources, employees' competences in the field of prevention and risk management in the enterprise should be constantly improved. This can be an important part of maintaining or improving risk management effectiveness (Agarwal & Rathod, 2006; Atkinson, 1999; Turner, 1993).

The latter is additionally important because, as shown by the analysis of environmental circumstances, Polish large and medium-sized enterprises specifically perceive the greatest threat in human resources, the errors and omissions of which may constitute a serious source of threats and losses. This confirms the results of research and analyses carried out so far in the area of the impact of employees' actions on the level of risk within the enterprise (Bevilacqua & Ciarapica, 2017; Skogdalen & Vinnem, 2011; Vaurio, 2009). The observations regarding the threat from the immediate environment, in particular from competitors and recipients, are also confirmed (Nudurupati et al., 2021; Gaganis et al., 2018; Prajogo, 2016; Rusten & Bryson, 2010; Sengupta, 2004; Cvitkovic, 1993). The surveyed enterprises perceive the greatest market threats in these two segments.

With regard to the distant environment, the most important source of risk for Polish managers are fluctuations in the economic situation resulting from the turbulence and volatility of modern economies described in theoretical chapters (Karagiannidis & Wilford, 2015). However, it is worth noting that during the research period the respondents did not perceive a significant threat from international crises which was most likely due to the domestic nature of their activities. In the current environment, in which the Chinese pandemic crisis has created a risk on an unprecedented scale and scope, this assessment could change (Rose, 2021; Gupta et al., 2021).

As part of the survey, Polish large and medium-sized enterprises also assessed the potential benefits of implementing risk management procedures. Their responses allowed us to define the practical dimensions of risk management effectiveness. And so, the vast majority of them quite firmly state that risk management contributes to the protection of the enterprise against threats and losses, i.e. it mitigates threats in the short-term operational perspective. A group of similar size also believes that risk management enables the enterprise to develop, i.e. it favours the achievement of long-term strategic goals. Importantly, Polish surveyed enterprises do not treat risk management as a way to survive (a much smaller number of responses), therefore they have a rational view of the effects of using risk management methods and tools.

8.2 Recommendations for Improving Risk Management Effectiveness

Obtained results of the questionnaire surveys allowed for the formulation of two groups of recommendations. The first one directly relates to the surveyed enterprises and is presented in Table 8.2. The second one is universal and it concerns the improvement of risk management effectiveness in the enterprise and is presented later in this section.

Based on the conducted observations and formulated research conclusions, it can be concluded that Polish large and medium-sized enterprises know the general principles of risk management. They also see a positive impact of risk management on the mitigation of threats and losses resulting from previous research (Klain & Reilley, 2021; Chen et al., 2019) and the creation of favourable (safe) development conditions in the long term. Nevertheless, the range of measures and methods used to manage risk should be considered modest and primarily based on one's own potential. Taking into account the fact that the effectiveness of risk management is most strongly influenced by the resource and methodological elements, in situations of serious market threats it may turn out that the protection applied by the surveyed enterprises is insufficient. For these reasons, most of the recommendations listed in Table 8.2 refer to the improvement of risk management methods and the extension of the scope of their use as well as to increasing the involvement of resources in the risk management process in the enterprise. Actions in these areas should positively affect the effectiveness of risk management analysed in the work.

It is also worth adding that the importance of risk management in the enterprise and the assessment of the effectiveness of actions taken in this area have certainly gained their importance due to the global, deep economic crisis caused by the Covid-19 pandemic (Huang & Liu, 2021). The scale and intensity of threats related to its occurrence and the effects that persist to this day have been a serious lesson in dealing with situations of above average economic risk for enterprises around the world. Many companies have not survived, many have found themselves in decline, and the long-term consequences of the pandemic will have a

Table 8.2 Recommendations arising from the general analysis of risk management determinants in Polish large and medium-sized enterprises

Group of determinants	Recommendations
Behavioural	Taking up new challenges conducive to the development of innovation and entrepreneurship, with properly prepared procedures for mitigating the excessive risk that may come with them. Being wary of excessive unjustified optimism that leads to disregard for threats.
Methodical	The use of risk management methods and tools even to a minimal extent in place of the lack of procedures in this area. More frequent use of prevention as a method of risk mitigation. Searching for other, new methods and tools to reduce threats and losses, apart from business insurance.
Resource	Including, at least ad hoc and periodic, external experts enabling an objective assessment of risk sources and control of procedures adopted as part of risk management in the enterprise. Involving employees in the risk management process to increase the effectiveness of activities in this area. Directing employees to training in the field of prevention. Training employees in the field of risk management, especially in the absence of an organisational department responsible for this process and not using the help of external entities. Attempting to organise the risk management process using internal resources in conditions of limited financial resources.
Environmental	Making employees aware of the sources of risk they generate, focusing on prevention. Conducting an analysis of competitiveness and looking for ways to strengthen it in order to mitigate risks related to recipients and competition. Monitoring and not underestimating the threats related to financial liquidity, the lack of which may lead to the bankruptcy of the enterprise. Preparation of a remedial plan in the event of a deep crisis and economic downturn. Monitoring and not disregarding the international environment in the event of rapid infestation and significant risk dispersion.

Source: Own work

negative impact on the activities of enterprises, industries and entire economies for a long time to come (Amankwah-Amoah et al., 2021; Dube et al., 2021; Khlystova et al., 2021; Wieczorek-Kosmala, 2021).

Effective risk management in the enterprise could most definitely contribute to the early identification of an impending threat and at least partially reduce the damage and losses associated with the impending crisis. Nevertheless, it is worth adding that without the support of the state, it would not be possible for many enterprises and industries to survive the pandemic (e.g. tourism, aviation or the food industry), because they have completely lost the ability to generate revenues, and thus a positive financial result (Groenewegen et al., 2021; Kobayashi et al., 2021; Łopatka & Fedorowicz, 2021). However, additional own protection within the early warning system or the risk management itself would certainly increase the effectiveness of crisis protection. Risk management is also an important element of enterprise security in the current post-pandemic situation in which there will still be business fluctuations, loss of customers or sales markets, i.e. those external threats that enterprises fear most. Hence, care for the proper identification, assessment, mitigation and control of risk should now be an important element of management in every enterprise.

General recommendations on risk management in an enterprise mainly refer to the observed model relationships defining the relationships between the identified groups of determinants and risk management effectiveness. They include the following insights:

1. Improving risk management effectiveness may be achieved by improving the methods and tools of risk management in the enterprise.
2. In this regard, it is recommended to use in-depth threats identyfication and assessment, and then to select a diversified mitigation instrumentation adjusted to individual risk sources.
3. Improving the effectiveness of risk management may also be achieved by increasing the involvement of resources in the risk management process.
4. Recommended in this regard is: the use of experts and external entities, and the participation of employees in risk management.

5. Risk management effectiveness can also be indirectly influenced by shaping the appropriate, desired attitudes of managers (eliminating fears of risk combined with confirming and extending knowledge about risk management methods).
6. Environmental circumstances related to the immediate and distant surroundings must be systematically monitored, paying particular attention to the most serious threats primarily posed by: recipients, competition and changes in the economic situation.
7. Enterprises should also use early warning systems to anticipate remedial action and develop crisis management plans that can be implemented in situations of sudden market failure such as the Covid-19 pandemic.

References

Agarwal, N., & Rathod, U. (2006). Defining 'success' for software projects: An exploratory revelation. *International Journal of Project Management, 24*(4), 358–370.

Amankwah-Amoah, J., Khan, Z., & Wood, G. (2021). COVID-19 and business failures: The paradoxes of experience, scale, and scope for theory and practice. *European Management Journal, 39*(2), 179–184.

Atkinson, R. (1999). Project management: Cost, time and quality, two best guesses and a phenomenon, it's time to accept other success criteria. *International Journal of Project Management, 17*(6), 337–342.

Bevilacqua, M., & Ciarapica, F. E. (2017). Human factor risk management in the process industry: A case study. *Reliability Engineering & System Safety, 169*, 149–159.

Brustbauer, J. (2016). Enterprise risk management in SMEs: Towards a structural model. *International Small Business Journal, 34*(1), 70–85.

Chen, Y.-L., Chuang, Y.-W., Huang, H.-G., & Shih, J.-Y. (2019). The value of implementing enterprise risk management: Evidence from Taiwan's financial industry. *The North American Journal of Economics and Finance, 54*, 100926.

Cui, Y., Sun, C., Xiao, H., & Zhao, C. (2016). How to become an excellent entrepreneur: The moderating effect of risk propensity on alertness to business ideas and entrepreneurial capabilities. *Technological Forecasting and Social Change, 112*, 171–177.

Cvitkovic, E. (1993). *Competition*. Palgrave Macmillan.
Dube, K., Nhamo, G., & Chikodzi, D. (2021). COVID-19 pandemic and prospects for recovery of the global aviation industry. *Journal of Air Transport Management, 92*, 102022.
Gaganis, C., Pasiouras, F., & Voulgari, F. (2018). Culture, business environment and SMEs' profitability: Evidence from European countries. *Economic Modelling, 78*, 275–292.
Groenewegen, J., Hardeman, S., & Stam, E. (2021). Does COVID-19 state aid reach the right firms? COVID-19 state aid, turnover expectations, uncertainty and management practices. *Journal of Business Venturing Insights, 16*, e00262.
Gupta, V., Santosh, K. C., Arora, R., Ciano, T., & Mohan, S. (2021). Socio-economic impact due to COVID-19: An empirical assessment. *Information Processing & Management, 102810*.
Hoogvelt, A., Puxty, A. G., Buckley, P. J., & Omarov, Y. (1987). *Multinational enterprise. An encyclopedic dictionary of concepts and terms*. Palgrave Macmillan.
Huang, S., & Liu, H. (2021). Impact of COVID-19 on stock price crash risk: Evidence from Chinese energy firms. *Energy Economics, 101*, 105431.
Karagiannidis, I., & Wilford, S. D. (2015). Modeling fund and portfolio risk: A bi-modal approach to analyzing risk in turbulent markets. *Review of Financial Economics, 25*, 19–26.
Khlystova, O., Kalyuzhnova, Y., & Belitski, M. (2021). The impact of the COVID-19 pandemic on the creative industries: A literature review and future research agenda. *Journal of Business Research, 139*, 1192–1210.
Klain, V. H., & Reilley, J. T. (2021). The temporal dynamics of enterprise risk management. *Critical Perspectives on Accounting, 102363*.
Kobayashi, Y., Heinrich, T., & Bryant, K. A. (2021). Public support for development aid during the COVID-19 pandemic. *World Development, 138*, 105248.
Łopatka, A., & Fedorowicz, K. (2021). Evaluation of the effectiveness of state aid offered to enterprises during the COVID-19 pandemic. *Procedia Computer Science, 192*, 4828–4836.
Mishra, P. K. (2020). COVID-19, Black Swan events and the future of disaster risk management in India. *Progress in Disaster Science, 8*, 100137.
Nudurupati, S. S., Garengo, P., & Bititci, U. S. (2021). Impact of the changing business environment on performance measurement and management practices. *International Journal of Production Economics, 232*, 107942.

Prajogo, D. I. (2016). The strategic fit between innovation strategies and business environment in delivering business performance. *International Journal of Production Economics, 171*, 241–249.

Rose, A. (2021). COVID-19 economic impacts in perspective: A comparison to recent U.S. disasters. *International Journal of Disaster Risk Reduction, 60*, 102317.

Rusten, G., & Bryson, J. (Eds.). (2010). *Industrial design, competition and globalization*. Palgrave Macmillan.

Sengupta, J. K. (2004). *Competition and growth*. Palgrave Macmillan.

Sengupta, J. K., & Fanchon, P. (2009). *Efficiency, market dynamics and industry growth*. Palgrave Macmillan.

Skogdalen, J. E., & Vinnem, J. E. (2011). Quantitative risk analysis offshore—Human and organizational factors. *Reliability Engineering & System Safety, 96*(4), 468–479.

Turner, J. R. (1993). *The handbook of project based management*. McGraw-Hill.

Vaurio, J. K. (2009). Human factors, human reliability and risk assessment in license renewal of a nuclear power plant. *Reliability Engineering & System Safety, 94*(11), 1818–1826.

Wang, C. M., Xu, B. B., Zhang, S. J., & Chen, Y. Q. (2016). Influence of personality and risk propensity on risk perception of Chinese construction project managers. *International Journal of Project Management, 34*(7), 1294–1304.

Wieczorek-Kosmala, M. (2021). COVID-19 impact on the hospitality industry: Exploratory study of financial-slack-driven risk preparedness. *International Journal of Hospitality Management, 94*, 102799.

Index

I. Jonek-Kowalska, *Effectiveness of Enterprise Risk Management*,
https://doi.org/10.1007/978-3-030-95376-8